Arthur T Fisher

Through the Stable And Saddle-Room

Arthur T Fisher

Through the Stable And Saddle-Room

ISBN/EAN: 9783744753180

Printed in Europe, USA, Canada, Australia, Japan

Cover: Foto ©ninafisch / pixelio.de

More available books at **www.hansebooks.com**

THROUGH THE STABLE

AND

SADDLE-ROOM

BY

ARTHUR T. FISHER

(*Late 21st Hussars*)

LONDON
RICHARD BENTLEY AND SON
Publishers in Ordinary to Her Majesty the Queen
1890

THE AUTHOR

DEDICATES THIS LITTLE BOOK

TO THE MEMORY OF HIS FRIEND AND COMMANDING OFFICER,

THE LATE

COLONEL E. B. WAKE,

21st Hussars.

June, 1890.

CONTENTS.

	PAGE
PREFACE	xvii

PART I.

STABLE AND STABLE GEAR.

CHAPTER I.

The stable.—Soil for situation.—Sand *v.* clay.—Points essential in the construction of stables.—Drainage.—Flooring — 3

CHAPTER II.

Ventilation.—Cavalry stables.—Argument in proof of the necessity for proper ventilation.—Anecdotes.—Autumn manœuvres of 1875 — 8

CHAPTER III.

Stable windows — 15

CHAPTER IV.

Warmth.—Material for outer walls.—Inside walls.—Roofing.—Thatched roofs — 18

CHAPTER V.

Space.—Water supply in stables.—Softening water.—
'Anti-calcaire.'—Precautions against fire.—Fire and
accident insurances.—Removing horses from a burning
stable - - - - - - - - 23

CHAPTER VI.

Stable doors.—Carelessness of grooms in leading horses
in and out of stables.—Good grooms *v.* bad - - 27

CHAPTER VII.

Stable fittings.—Stalls.—Loose-boxes.—Stall partitions.
—Government stable fittings.—Wood for partitions.—
—Racks and mangers.—Feeding on the ground.—
Movable fittings.—Fork and broom racks.—Shelves.
—Stall-post pegs.—Dust and dirt.—Slovenly servants - 30

CHAPTER VIII.

Stable necessaries.—Pillar-reins.—Necessity for looping
up pillar-reins.—Accidents from loose pillar-reins.—
List of grooming utensils.—List of stable utensils.—
Brushes.—Work done by the blind.—Body-brushes.—
Water-brushes. — Dandy-brushes. — Curry-combs.—
Mane-combs. — Sponges. — Hoof-pickers. — Stable-
rubbers. — Chamois leathers. — Burnishers. — Saddle-
soap.—Clipping-machines.—Singeing-lamps.—Stable-
scissors.—Average prices of grooming utensils.—Stable
brooms.—Wheelbarrows.—Buckets.—Stable lamps and
lighting.—Candle-ends.—Corn-measures. — Corn-sieves.
—Corn-bins.—Prices of corn-bins.—Average price of
stable utensils - - - - - - - 37

CHAPTER IX.

Horse-clothing and horses' coats.—Kerseymere clothing.—Colour of clothing.—Making up of clothing.—London and provincial work.—Quarter-sheet and breast-piece.—Fillet-strings.—Pad and roller.—Improper girthing up of rollers.—Evils of girthing up of rollers too tightly.—Hoods.—Short hoods.—Fawn-striped rugs.—Weight and price of ditto.—How to test woollen goods.—Night rugs.—Summer clothing - - - - 54

CHAPTER X.

Bandages.—Mode of tying bandages.—Cracked heels.—Woollen bandages.—Hunting bandages.—Support from bandages.—Colour of material for bandages.—Care of bandages.—'Naphthaline' for prevention of moth in woollen goods, etc.—'Naphthaline' for saddles.—Stocking bandages.—Water bandages.—Chamois-leather bandages.—Sweating bandages.—Bandaging.—Prices of bandages - - - - - 64

CHAPTER XI.

Stable headstalls.—Prices of headstalls.—Lead-lines.—Logs.—Fitting of lead-lines.—Prices of lead-lines.—Prices quoted for articles.—Good and bad articles.—Rack-chains.—Spring-hooks.—New patent hooks.—Kneecaps.—Use of kneecaps.—Evils of kneecaps.—Proper description of kneecaps.—Kneecaps too tightly fitted.—How to fit on kneecaps.—Necessity for obtaining good articles.—Price of kneecaps.—Watering bridles.—Watering snaffles.—Dirty watering snaffles.—Reins for watering snaffles.—Care and condition of watering snaffles.—Accidents from rotten reins.—Mode of fitting watering-bridle reins.—Leading-reins.—Useful maxims.—Exercising without saddles.—Price of watering bridles - - - - - - - 71

PART II.

COACHHOUSE AND SADDLE-ROOM.

CHAPTER XII.

Coachhouse.—Heating coachhouse.—Watering floor of coachhouse. — Flooring of coachhouse.— Saddle-room. —Doors of saddle-room. — Stove of saddle-room.— Patent stove.—Light from window of saddle-room.— Panelling walls of saddle-room.—Disposal of saddlery in saddle-room. — Saddle-racks. — Own patent saddle-racks. — Construction of saddle-racks. — Advantage of saddle-racks. — Prices of saddle-racks. — Saddle-room shelves.—Saddle-room cupboards.—Order and cleanliness.—Forage store.—Disposal of forage in store.—Economy of order.—Bedding-sheds.—Economy and construction of bedding-sheds.—Grooms' chambers.—Communicating window from grooms' chambers to stable.—Comfort of servants' rooms.—Cleanliness of servants' rooms.—Inspection of servants' rooms by master   -   -   -   -   -   -   - 87

CHAPTER XIII.

Requirements of a good saddle.—Parts of a saddle.—Saddle-trees.—Saddle-seats.—Saddle-fittings. — Saddle-flaps. — Stuffing of saddles. — Panels. — Sweat-flaps.—Good and bad trees.—Cut of saddles.—Straight seats. —Argument in favour of straight seats.—Length of rein obtained by use of straight seats.—Why horses pull less when ridden by ladies.—Knee-rolls *v.* plain flaps.—*Field* correspondence as to knee-rolls and plain flaps.—Use of the leg in riding.—Cavalry riding.—Advantage of knee-rolls.—Major Whyte-Melville on plain flaps.— —Girths.—Stirrup-irons.—Saddle-bar stops.—Fitting of stirrup-leathers. — Good saddles. — Best saddles.—Materials used for lining saddles.—Messrs. Whippy's new system of lining saddles.—Saddle-heads.—Numnabs. — Chambering saddles. — Side-saddles and sore backs.—Back-stays.—Cause and prevention of sore backs in ladies' horses.—Proper position for a lady on side-saddle. — Improper seat. — Safety stirrups for ladies - - - - - - - 101

CHAPTER XIV.

Bridles. — Headstalls. — Buckles. — Browbands. — Reins. —Parts of a bridle.—Double-rein snaffles.—Bits.— Shape of a horse's mouth.—Hard and soft mouths.— Spoiled mouths.—How to fit a bit in a horse's mouth.— Curb.—Throat-lash.—Noseband.—Variety of bits.— The temptation of a saddler's shop.—Fancy bits.— Useful bits. — Useless bits. — Snaffles. — Use of two snaffles.—Gag-snaffles.—Bits and bridoons.—Too severe bits.—The grid-iron.—Curb-save.—Lip-straps.—Ward-bits.—Bit-mouthpieces.—Instrument for measuring a horse's mouth.—The 'Pelham' bit.—'Ben Morgan' bit.—'Ben Morgan' bit for driving.—Breast-plates.— Fitting of breast-plates. — Martingales. — Standing martingales.—Rein-rings.—How to saddle a horse.— Cleaning of saddlery.—Evils of saddle-paste.—Care in cleaning saddle-flaps.—Prices of saddlery - - 129

CHAPTER XV.

Harness. — Parts of harness. — Headstall. — Bit. — Bridoon-hangers. — Buckles. — Harness furniture. — Metal browbands.—Evils of old-fashioned driving-bit.— 'Liverpool' bits.—Sliding ports.—Use of bit-bars.— Blinkers.—Crest-brushes.—Collars.—Hames.—Hames-rings.—Saddle-terrets.—Danger of bearing-rein hooks. —Back-band.—Tugs.—Belly-band.—'Tilbury' tugs.— Crupper.—Breeching.—Traces.—Spare traces.—Kicking-straps.—Reins.—Billets.—Use and abuse of bearing-reins.—Harness-cleaning, black and brown.—Brass-work.—How to clean patent leather.—Harness-cleaning utensils and prices.—How to harness a horse to a carriage.—How to unharness a horse from a carriage.—Double harness.—Roller-bolts.—Uses of pole.—Pole-chains.—Coupling-reins.—Fitting of coupling-reins.—Carriages.—Horse and carriage to be suitably proportioned.—Care of carriages.—Varnish must be dry.—Abuse of the spoke-brush.—How to clean a carriage.—Water-hose.—Wheel-lift.—Use and abuse of wheel-lift.—Care of carriage-poles.—Care of wheels.—Tramway lines.—Evil effects of sun on a carriage.—List and prices of carriage-cleaning utensils - - - - 152

PART III.

FEEDING AND FARRIERY.

CHAPTER XVI.

Forage.—Hay.—Average price of hay.—Weight of hay.—Meadow-hay.—Old *v.* new hay.—Selection of hay.—Perfect hay.—Mow-burnt hay.—How to test quality of hay.—Rye-grass and clover.—Oats.—English and foreign oats.—Black, white, and gray oats.—Weight of oats.—Testing weight of oats.—Price of oats.—Old oats.—Made-up oats.—How to detect made-up oats.—How to select oats.—Weighing oats.—Straw.—Varieties of straw.—Foreign competition.—Price of straw.—Oat-straw.—Bedding.—Fern.—Sawdust.—Peat-mould.—Moss-litter.—Bran.—Price of bran - - - 175

CHAPTER XVII.

Extra forage.—Beans.—Price of beans.—Quantity and effects of beans.—Peas.—Price of peas.—Maize.—Use of maize.—Price of maize.—Linseed.—Linseed-mashes.—Merits of linseed-mashes.—Linseed-oil.—Cooked foods.—Advantages of cooked foods.—Effects of cooked foods.—Preparation of cooked foods.—Green forage.—

Quantity of green forage to be given.—Lucerne.—
Carrots.—Price of carrots.—Quantity of food required
for a horse.—Daily scale of food.—Cost of horse-keep.
—Annual cost of horse-keep.—Feeding horses.—Chaff.
—Indigestion. — Hay and straw for chaff. — Feeding-
hours. — Feeding with hay. — Watering. — Food and
work. — Bad feeders. — Instinct. — Coaxing delicate
feeders.—Mice in stable.—Rock-salt.—Bran-mashes.—
How to make bran-mashes.—Bran-poultices.—Linseed-
poultices.—How to make linseed-poultices.—Gruel.—
How to make gruel.—Ale for tired horse.—An English
sportsman - - - - - - 188

CHAPTER XVIII.

Personal supervision by master.—Such personal super-
vision not lowering.—Evidences of a good groom.—
Amount of work for one servant.—Overworked grooms.
—Good servants procurable.—A fair day's work and a
fair day's wage.—Hours for grooming.—Time required
to clean a horse.—Blind horses and summer coats.—
'Wolf-teeth' and shying.—Hour for 'morning' stables.
—Hours for, and routine of, grooming.—Morning.—
Mid-day. — Evening. — Grooming a tired hunter. —
—Extra rules for grooming hunters.—Refusing corn.—
Points to be specially attended to in grooming.—How
to test good grooming.—How to groom.—The use of
the curry-comb. — Clipping. — Time for clipping. —
Singeing. — Naphtha and gas singeing-lamps. — Un-
clipped legs.—Treatment after singeing.—Mane-pulling.
—How to pull a mane.—Hogging manes.—Tail-cutting.
Docking - - - - - - - 205

CHAPTER XIX.

Shoeing.—Odd feet indicative of previous unsoundness.
—Construction of foot.—Shape and structure of crust
and sole.—The frog.—Thickness of crust and sole.—

Ahæ of coffin-bone.—Circular action of foot.—Use of shoes.—Iron suitable for shoes.—Sole not to be pared.—Ignorance of farriers.—Evils of chopping out the heels.—Lowering the feet.—Shoe to rest on the crust.—Shape and thickness of shoe.—Clinches.—Position of nails.—Concave shoes.—'Fitzwygram' shoes.—The 'Charlier' system.—Tips.—Roughing.—Patent hoof-pads.—Calkins.—Over-reaching.—Cause of cutting and prevention.—Bevelled shoes.—Inconvenience caused by neglect of servants.—Inspection by farrier.—Shoeing-pricks.—Price of shoeing.—Hot feet and remedy.—Stopping.—Recipe for stopping.—Thrush and treatment.—Corns and treatment.—Shoeing with leather.—Lameness.—Shoulder lameness.—Lameness in hock.—From splint.—Of fetlock-joint.—Sandcrack and treatment.—Hoof-ointment - - - - - 224

PART IV.

AILMENTS AND THEIR TREATMENT.

CHAPTER XX.

Mud-fever.—How to prevent mud-fever.—Cold and cough.—Prevention of cold and cough.—Treatment for cold and cough.—Strangles.—Treatment for strangles.—Glanders and farcy.—Malignity of glanders.—Difference between roaring and broken wind.—Roaring and its causes.—Whistling.—New cure for roaring.—Horses subject to roaring.—Broken wind.—Treatment for broken wind.—Wind-sucking and crib-biting.—Wind-sucking and crib-biting not infectious.—Weaving.—String-halt.—Worms.—Cure for worms.—Bots.—Eating bedding.—Muzzles.—Price of muzzles.—Tearing clothing.—Prevention of tearing clothing.—Kicking in stable.—Prevention of kicking in stable.—Capped hock.—Treatment for capped hock.—

Capped elbow.—Treatment for capped elbow.—Cause of capped elbow.—Prevention of capped elbow.—Cracked heels.—Cure of cracked heels.—Windgalls.—Treatment for windgalls. — Spavin. — Treatment of spavin. — Thoroughpin.—Curb.—Treatment of curb.—Ringbone. — Treatment of ringbone. — Side-bones. — Splint. — Treatment of splint. — 'Periosteotomy.' — Causes of splint.—Speedy-cut.—Cause of speedy-cut.—Treatment of speedy-cut.—Navicular disease.—Seat of navicular disease.—Unnerving for navicular disease.—Navicular disease hereditary.—Peculiarity of navicular disease.—Indication of disease.—Detection of disease.—Effect of sympathy. — Sore backs and galls. — Examination of back.—Treatment for sore backs.—Sitfast.—Treatment of sitfast.—Lampas.—Treatment of lampas.—Toothache. — 'High-blowing.' — Ringworm.—Treatment for ringworm.—Preparation for physic.—How to give a ball. — Physic after grass. — Purging. — Treatment. — Diseases of the eye.—Cataract.—Causes of blindness.—Blind coach-horses.—Examination for cataract - - 257

CHAPTER XXI.

Recipe for physic-balls. — Recipe for cleaning leather breeches.—Recipe for cleaning white cords.—Recipe for cleaning brown cords.—Recipe for cleaning top-boots.—Recipe for cleaning scarlet coats.—Recipe for cleaning drab coats.—Recipe for cleaning hunting-hats 290

CHAPTER XXII.

Livery.—Vulgar liveries.—Leather waist-belts.—Pad-grooms.—Equipment for pad-grooms.—Riding-clothes.—Advice as to the purchase of a horse.—Engagement-form for men-servants.—Finale - - - - 293

PREFACE.

So many books have been written on horses and stable management, that in commencing the present little work I feel that I am but about to traverse ground which has been '*over*-trodden'—nay, 'churned up'—by those who have been in the field before me, and that the subject is already too well worn to admit of yet *another* treatise upon it being produced. I hope, however, that such may prove *not* to be the case, inasmuch as since it is indisputable that no two people entertain *quite* the same ideas on any subject, I may be able, I trust, to view the one at present before me, and treat the same, in a somewhat different manner to my predecessors. What has invariably struck me in perusing the many books on horses and their management which have been already before the public is, as a rule, their want of *simplicity*. They appear to me to be rather mystifying than instructive. There is usually a great deal said about the horse, his breeding and origin, etc., and a great deal of what may be termed veterinary information, the latter often very old-fashioned and well-nigh obsolete; but there is a want of useful explanation requisite for a person who is utterly ignorant of such matters, and by which the daily routine of ordinary stable management should be carried on, as well, I may add, as the why and the wherefore for such routine—why such a thing is the *right* way, and such the *wrong*.

It is for this class of persons—the altogether ignorant, those who know absolutely nothing about horses and stables—that I desire to write, and to impart the information which I consider that the experience of a lifetime spent amongst horses, including many years of service in an English cavalry regiment, coupled with an ever-earnest desire to gather and store up all knowledge regarding the management of the animal I love so well, entitle me to offer for their help and guidance.

Every true Englishman loves a horse, even if he knows no more about him than he does about a kangaroo, and but few of our countrymen can gaze on a handsome horse without admiration; and if questioned and answering truthfully regarding his knowledge of horses, would, if ignorant, admit his want of knowledge somewhat blushingly, as if he were ashamed to say he knew nothing about them. His blushes be to his credit! How *should* he know if he has never had the opportunity of learning? Yet that man may shortly afterwards find himself in the possession of a horse which choice or necessity, or both, has made his property. He is entirely in the hands of his groom. The latter is perhaps careless or dishonest, and then commences a long course of experience dearly bought, and what should have been to him a source of pleasure and, *at least, convenience*, if not of profit (as in the case of a professional man whose requirements necessitate his keeping a stable), becomes too often a very bugbear of worry, annoyance and expense. He buys a book on horses, and sits down to read up the subject steadily and honestly. He learns, perhaps, how the Darley Arabian, etc., influenced our English breed; and then commencing a chapter on age and teeth, gets into a hopeless muddle, which a further chapter on anatomy renders a complete quagmire. His horse is perhaps slightly ailing, and the veterinary surgeon has run him up a long bill and made out a long 'case' out of nothing; and meanwhile his groom, having little or no work to do, is enjoying himself with his friends in the nearest pot-house, while the services of the jobmaster have to be requisitioned. He looks again into his book and tries to study up the ailment from which his horse is suffering. If lucky enough to find any mention of it, he very soon comes to the conclusion that it is beyond him altogether. He can't understand all the scientific terms and long names given, and so he shies the book away, and begins to think that he will stick to the jobmaster in future; and perhaps his decision is not an unwise one after all. But his *interest* in his horse has gone. He cares nothing for the jobmaster or *his* horses: they don't belong to *him*, and so long as they draw or carry him about he is satisfied. And so his dream of any pleasure to be derived from a stable of his own has vanished, and all for the want of a little knowledge, which he would *gladly* gain if he only knew where to obtain it. It is this *little* knowledge I wish to impart: just enough to enable a man to manage his stable with the 'eye of a master,' and to protect himself from the troubles caused by the carelessness and dishonesty of his servants; to make his stable a pleasure to him, and to keep his horses fit to look at and fit to work. I aim at nothing more, and if my efforts prove successful in any *one single* instance, I shall feel that they have not been *quite* wasted.

THROUGH STABLE AND SADDLE-ROOM.

PART I.
STABLE AND STABLE-GEAR.

CHAPTER I.

The stable.—Soil for situation.—Sand *v.* clay.—Points essential in the construction of stables.—Drainage.—Flooring.

I PROPOSE to go through my subject systematically, and to divide it into the following parts, viz. :

Part I.—The Stable and Stable-Gear.
Part II.—The Coach-house and Saddle-room.
Part III.—Feeding and Farriery.
Part IV.—Ailments, and their Treatment.
Miscellaneous.

I will take the stable first of all, arguing that it is no use to purchase a horse unless you have somewhere to put him, and that somewhere is suitable for his accommodation. I will try and describe what a *perfect* stable should be like. One can hardly expect to obtain *perfection* in anything; but with the perfect model in front of us, it will be, perhaps, easier to recognise the main points to be sought for and secured, if possible.

We will begin at the *situation*. This latter should, I need hardly say, be dry, sheltered, and light, and, if possible, *not* on a clay soil. The different soils come in this order :

    Sand, 1.   Chalk, 3.
    Gravel, 2.   Clay, 4.

I have, you see, placed clay the *last*.

In a sandy or gravelly soil water is generally good, apart from the natural dryness of such soils; and the quality of water has a very marked effect on the well-being of horses, and here, although chalk, as a *soil*, is better than clay, still it must be admitted that the water from the latter, being less hard than that from the former, is more suitable for horses; nevertheless, no animals thrive as well on clay as on chalk, and it is an indisputed fact that where kennels are situated on a clay soil young hounds are never so thriving as on any other kind of soil. I therefore consider that clay must take a 'back seat'; but on whatever soil stables may be placed, they should on no account, if *possible*, be situated in a dip or hollow. Common-sense argues too strongly against their being so; albeit, too often such is the case—in many instances dryness being sacrificed to the shelter afforded by a hill-side. Shelter and warmth are doubtless necessary,

SOIL FOR SITUATION.

and *very* necessary, but *dryness* is of the first importance. The horse is a native of a dry, sandy country, and it may be noticed that in districts where horses are bred, those in which the soil is of either of the first-named three, or of a good loam, are of better constitution, and their bone is of better quality. Take, for example, the Yorkshire and Lincolnshire breeds. The former are, as a rule, not so well boned as the latter. The bone is not so dense; it is softer, more liable to throw out exostoses (splints, etc.) than that of the latter horses. The counties, though adjoining, are different in soil: the former is clay, the latter sandy and lighter. In my opinion a good Lincolnshire horse is the best horse in the world, bar *none*. A horse can stand a good deal of cold and thrive fairly well, as our mountain ponies prove to be the case; but a low-lying, damp, clayey soil is most detrimental to his well-doing.

Having selected a suitable site for the stable, the next thing to be considered is its construction.

Here the main points to be considered are these:

Drainage.   Warmth.
Ventilation.   Space.
Light.   Water supply.

Drainage is perhaps the one chief thing of all

which must be absolutely *perfect*; and bear in mind that unless a drain *is perfect* it is *no drain at all*; the word is then a misnomer.

The simpler the system the better. An open ditch is better than an elaborately covered subway.

Let the drains from each stall or box run direct into one common gutter, which traverses the stable from one end to the other, and the further this gutter is extended beyond the stable in its open form before it is received into any underground drain the better. As far as *stable* drainage is concerned nothing further is necessary.

The flooring of each stall or box should be of some material which will not easily break, and for this purpose there is nothing better than the hard blue bricks which are made for the purpose, and which are scored with lines at regular intervals each way, to allow of the passage of fluid; these are each one in itself a small drain, and when the stall is brushed down the broom completely cleans each one out; but the flooring of the stable generally should be on a concrete base, by which means the level is preserved in each stall. At the same time it is absolutely essential that the bricks should be well and evenly laid and joined with *cement*, and placed so that the lines cut in the bricks correspond with each other.

The flooring of the stalls should slope very slightly inwards towards the centre, and also towards the gutter or 'gangway,' as it is termed. It is far too often the case that the slope is too great. If so, undue strain is placed on the horses' hocks, and horses will, in order to avoid thus having to stand, as it were, uphill, draw back on to the gangway as far as their lead-lines will admit, and get into the habit of bearing on their head-stalls, to the detriment of the latter and their own health, to say nothing of making the gangway dirty, etc.

CHAPTER II.

Ventilation. — Cavalry stables. — Argument in proof of the necessity for proper ventilation. — Anecdotes — Autumn manœuvres of 1875.

If it is necessary to lay stress on the subject of drainage, it is scarcely less so regarding that of ventilation. If drainage should be perfect, ventilation should be equally so.

Now, *perfect* ventilation means perfect freedom from draught, contradictory as the assertion may at first sight appear to be. In other words, there should be in a stable every facility for the ingress of *fresh* air and the egress of *foul*—and yet this should be arranged so as to secure to the inmates of that stable complete immunity from what is commonly called *draught*. The incoming of the fresh, and exit of the foul air, should be insensibly and rapidly effected.

To ensure this is a simple matter enough, provided it is done in the right way. There should be one or more (according to the size of the stable) ventilating shafts in the roof itself, and one or more *on each side* of the stable, near the top of the walls. These should have what is termed 'louvre boards,' and cords to allow of their being opened or closed, wholly or partially, as desired. Furthermore, there should be ventilating gratings a few inches from the floor on all the walls, and these should also be furnished with closing bars, so that they can be kept open or shut.

As far as the ventilators are concerned, nothing further is necessary, other than the common sense to use them properly, and to regulate them according to weather—but it is needless to add that *some* of these must be ever open, day and night. It is but a matter for very ordinary intelligence to determine which should be closed.

I think that the present is no inopportune time to enlarge somewhat on the evils of bad and insufficient ventilation, and the benefits to be derived from the reverse. Much sickness would be prevented in stables if more attention were paid to ventilation than is far too generally the case. Now, a horse consumes a large quantity of air in the twenty-four hours—far more than people suppose, judging from the size of the stables which one so often sees, their imperfect arrangement, and the absence of a proper (often of any) system of ventilation.

Without the requisite supply of fresh air it is *impossible* to maintain horses in perfect health and condition.

The wilful, pigheaded ignorance of grooms in this respect is proverbial. They are so afraid that the horses under their charge will catch cold, and that their coats will 'stare,' as it is termed, that they invariably stop up every crevice and ventilator in a stable in cold weather, thereby thinking to secure the end they have in view, whereas they are, all the time, but taking the most certain steps to ensure the very evil they would avert.

It is a well-known, and I may say an undisputed, fact (by all who know anything about the subject) that horses (young horses especially), on coming *into* stables *from* grass, are nearly always affected with throat, and often with lung, ailments, in a greater or less degree ; while assuming the reverse to be the case, and they are moved *from* stables *to* *grass*, they rarely, if ever, suffer from the change, thus proving how absolutely essential pure air is to their well-doing.

Despite all that has from time to time been advanced on this subject, excepting in large establishments a well and properly ventilated stable seems to be the exception rather than the rule; and there are many of the *larger* establishments, which I could name if I chose, where such details are very unduly cared for, and the ventilation is by no means what it should be, although the fittings, etc., of the stable may be very smart and lavishly carried out in other respects, and the horses' names painted up in gold letters, etc., and all that style of thing. I have very often, in such cases, been well-nigh stifled with the overloaded atmosphere.

I must admit that very many of our cavalry stables (I do not, of course, allude to the more modern-built ones, but to those of older date) are almost infamous as regards their construction, and it is impossible to keep the horses in health unless every door and window is kept open. They are very often low, dark, badly paved, ill-drained, narrow-stalled places, and nothing but the very greatest care prevents their becoming literal hot-beds of disease. True it is that, of the more modern ones, many are equally excellent in every respect, and save where a contract has been badly carried out as regards the quality of the material used for doors, windows, and other fittings, they are for the most part almost perfect.

Of those which have come under my own

particular experience, I should give the preference to the new cavalry stables at Glasgow and Colchester, which far surpass, the former especially, any cavalry stables I have ever seen. Those at Glasgow are magnificent. It may perhaps be interesting, in further proof of the value of an unlimited supply of fresh air in stables, to quote the following facts :

In cavalry regiments, the young horses which are purchased as 'remounts' are chiefly obtained in Ireland, and these come over thence in batches varying in number as they are required. They are packed in cattle-trucks, and started on their journey, and often have to travel in severe weather with no other protection from the cold than their own coats; yet on their arrival few, as a rule, seem any the worse for it, beyond fatigue and accidents, the result of kicks, etc., and it is very rarely, if ever, that they are affected with coughs or colds. They are nearly all brought straight from grass, yet, within a few days of their being placed in stables, and with every precaution taken to ensure ventilation (the doors and windows of the stables being left open day and night, and but very few being placed in each stable), they nearly all suffer from coughs and colds, which generally end in strangles.

During the autumn manœuvres of 1875, I was,

with my own regiment and two other cavalry regiments, encamped for some ten days in a place called Colony Bog, near Aldershot. It was a time to be ever ruefully remembered by all who took part in them, by reason of its cheerless, wet misery; for during the ten days we were there, I can most truthfully assert that it rained almost incessantly day and night, and what, even in a dry summer, was always more or less of a 'bog' became a 'lake.' Until we had been there for some days, exposed to all this inclemency of the weather, the horses had not so much as even a single blanket to cover them, and yet, notwithstanding this exposure, though it is true they were affected by the cold and wet (and it *was* cold and wet) in other ways, colds and coughs were unheard of.

Again, at the same time, an officer of my regiment had of necessity to take out with him into camp (he being at the time short of horses) an old and favourite charger, which, at the time of her going out from the stables in barracks, was suffering from a severe cold. In a few days she was quite well again.

Another friend of mine, a captain in another regiment, was, on his first going out with us into camp, suffering from an acute attack of neuralgia, but he was quite well in less than twenty-four hours after he had arrived there. Nor did I hear of anyone suffering from coughs or colds, though we hardly knew what it was to feel really dry during the whole time we were out, and we were forced to put our clothes into our beds to try and keep them dry during the night.

Now, these are plain facts, the truth of which all those who were there present with me can vouch for, and there must be many other similar cases which could be adduced in further proof of what I say. If people would but give their horses a chance of breathing the air they should breathe, and which is so essential for them, they would save themselves much anxiety and expense consequent upon the frequent visits of the veterinary surgeon, and their horses would be more 'fit to look at' and more 'fit to go' than is but too often the case.

CHAPTER III.

Stable windows.

NEXT to the ventilation, I suppose that the lighting of a stable ought to be considered.

In this much must depend on the situation of the stable. The latter should, where it is practicable, face south or south-west, so as to obtain as much sunlight as possible. Light is as essential to the well-doing of horses as air and warmth; and in that they are not different to the rest of the creation; but the light which is supplied to a stable through the windows should be admitted so as not to be a source of annoyance to the horses. Nothing could well be more so than for the latter to have to face the glare of the sun shining upon them through a glass window. I should, therefore, select the southern side, *i.e.*, the side *opposite* to that on which the mangers are situated, for the windows of a stable. It is very easy to shade them in hot weather by means of blinds or screens, and in winter the maximum of light is secured.

The windows of a stable should be made to fit *very* carefully and well, and should be arranged so as to take out altogether if required, and to open on a pivot rather than by means of the ordinary cords and pulleys, which latter are for ever getting out of order. A *lattice* window is to my way of thinking preferable to one made of large squares of glass; the glass used may be either plain, or ground, or coloured. Stable windows are constantly getting broken, and the lattice windows are very much more easily and cheaply repaired than the others; and where there is ample light to be obtained, I should prefer their adoption, and I like their appearance better. Where there is a difficulty in procuring sufficient light by reason of surrounding buildings, etc., the ordinary modern style is of course necessary.

There should, however, be not less than one window to every three horses, unless it be an extra large one. If it is necessary to have the windows placed on the side of the stable which *faces* the horses, they should be arranged so as to be as high up as they can be conveniently situated, and must then be opened by means of cords or a wand made for the purpose; but wherever they may be, the *side* walls are unsuitable for them, and every facility should be given for their being easily cleaned and kept free from the dust which so quickly accumulates in a stable ; and dust and dirt are two things which should never be allowed to remain in a stable longer than they would be in a drawing-room ; but of this I will speak later on.

CHAPTER IV.

Warmth.—Material for outer walls.—Inside walls.—Roofing.
—Thatched roofs.

In the second chapter I made mention of the following points as necessary in the construction of stables, viz., drainage, ventilation, light, warmth, space, and water supply. I have briefly dealt with the first three, and that of warmth claims our next attention. In speaking of warmth in a stable, I do not wish the reader to infer that I at all advocate an over-high temperature ; I rather desire to impress upon him the necessity there is to *avoid* such. I should, perhaps, have better expressed myself if I had used the word 'temperature.' However, the former term carries with it the fuller meaning, and so I have decided to retain it, and the reader will see in what manner I propose to deal with it, and why I have determined upon its use.

We have, as I have said, selected a site for our

stable, and determined upon the best aspect for it
—its base and flooring, its drainage, its ventilation, and its lighting, but I have as yet said
nothing regarding the actual construction of its
walls. Now, I suppose that out of every dozen
stables, at least two-thirds of them are built of
bricks. Where stone is scarce, and consequently
expensive, there is no alternative but to use some
other material. Of those which are more readily
to hand, bricks, I suppose, are, as a rule, the most
easily obtainable. Of course, they are very inferior
to good stone, by reason of their being more porous.
It is stated that a brick will absorb a pint of
water. If that is true, what, then, can be less
suited for building purposes, inasmuch as a brick
building must necessarily absorb a very great
amount of moisture? Where, however, they are
used, it is essential that the building should be
the very best of its kind possible, and by the
means of *double* walls every precaution taken to
ensure the inside of the stable being as dry as
possible. Unless this *is* so (and such a building is
necessarily somewhat costly at first), a good wooden
building, or one of corrugated iron lined with wood,
and the space between packed with sawdust or some
such non-conducting material, is far superior in my
estimation, inasmuch as dryness and more equable

temperature are better maintained. In stables especially, where such is easily obtainable, flint and stone appear to me to be *excellent*, nor can I think that there *can* be anything *better* suited for the purpose; and it has the advantage of being very enduring and pleasant to look at, and, I should say, is as well-nigh impervious to damp as it can be.

An equable temperature is what should be considered as of the first importance in a stable, and it is *impossible* to maintain such if the building itself is composed of thin walls of a porous texture.

Of whatever substance the walls of a stable may be, they should be lined inside. For this purpose cement *painted* is the best. I do not say that I like its *appearance* as well as a wooden matchboarding; but it is, I think, healthier and cleaner, and more easily kept clean, than woodwork. It is also safer, not only from being uninflammable, but also because, in the case of a horse kicking, there is no danger from splinters of wood, etc., and it offers less inducement for a horse to gnaw and contract the vice of crib-biting. I am myself a strong advocate for as little woodwork as possible being used inside a stable, for these reasons. As regards the cemented walls being healthier there can be no *possible* doubt, as it is obvious that woodwork would be more likely to retain impurities.

We now come to the question of roof, and as to whether it is better to have the forage-loft over the stable or not. I consider that it *is*; but where such is *not* the case there should be a ceiling, and (if in the country) a *thatched* roof. A roof made of thatch, if *well* done, will last for many years with but a very small annual outlay. The *only* objection I have to its use is the possibility of its catching fire. I therefore should not use it in a town, but in the country the case is different. As is well known, a thatched roof is warmer in winter and cooler in summer, and an equable temperature is more easily maintained. There is no denying that its appearance is in its favour. A good Dorsetshire thatcher (and the Dorset people understand the business better than any other labourers) can put on a roof which will last a lifetime, and which is as regular and level as a roof of any other material. I must, however, caution the reader against using a thatched roof unless he can secure the services of a *really good* thatcher. A bad thatch is perhaps the worst roof in the world, whereas a good one is amongst the very best. Next to thatch, a stone or tiled roof is to be preferred. Slate roofs are for ever getting out of order, and their appearance is also against them, and when they are loosened by heavy gales, etc., they are apt to be uncommonly dangerous, and to rip off very rapidly.

However, as 'circumstances alter cases,' so I will leave the matter in the hands of the reader to judge for himself as to which (if he has any choice in the matter) to select.

CHAPTER V.

Space.—Water supply in stables.—Softening water.—'Anti-calcaire.'—Precautions against fire.—Fire and accident insurances.—Removing horses from a burning stable.

THE subject of space must necessarily go hand-in-hand with that of construction.

If I were asked how large a stable for so many horses should be, my reply would be: As large as possible, within the limits of reason; and I could not say more if I were to write for a year on the subject. Plenty of height, width, and depth. Ground space and money must, however, both be limited, but a stable should be always larger than is *absolutely* necessary; that is to say, where one horse only is likely to be kept there should be room for two; where two, room for three; and where three or four, room for five or six, and so on in like proportion. The extra accommodation is always useful, and the increased air-space most desirable. As I intend to go more fully into the subject of stalls, loose-boxes, etc., later on, I will not enter upon it here. It is but necessary to bear in mind that it is an absolute impossibility to keep horses in health if they are overcrowded. By giving them plenty of space, and maintaining a proper system of ventilation—due regard being paid to their own cleanliness, and that of their surroundings, good food, good water, good drainage, and *plenty* of work—everything, barring accidents, will be almost sure to go well; but no amount of care and trouble will answer the purpose if they are overcrowded. Sooner or later the evil will become apparent. The man who is the possessor of one horse only generally contrives to get more work out of that one than his neighbour who may have three or four. Very much, it is true, because that one is better cared for, perhaps, and *gets* plenty of work, and also because the chances are that, his stable being probably built to accommodate two, there is no overcrowding, and consequently there is more breathing-space.

As regards the water supply of stables, it must be *good* and sufficient. A tap, both inside as well as outside, is a great convenience, and where the one is possible the other is equally so, and costs but little more. Where, however, the water has to be obtained by means of a pump, then a water-trough, or a receptacle to hold the water which is pumped up, should be at hand, inasmuch as it is ever a good thing for the water to remain in the air for some time after it has been drawn, and this very much softens it, and renders it more suitable for drinking than when it is drawn fresh from the pump. But such trough or vessel must, it is needless to say, be kept scrupulously clean and changed frequently, and should once a week at least be scrubbed with salt to prevent any furring of the sides and bottom. Where the water is *especially* hard, it may be softened by the use of the material sold nowadays under the name of 'Anti-calcaire,' which is most effective and very moderate in price. A small quantity can be kept mixed up in a barrel, and taken out for daily use.

As I have before remarked, *very* hard water is not suitable for horses, and it should invariably be softened by some such means as I have mentioned. Exposure to the air is very efficacious in most instances; but there *are* cases in which even *this* precaution is barely sufficient, and so recourse must be had to some other means, and from all I have heard of 'Anti-calcaire,' it is, I am assured on the *very best* authority, all it professes to be. It is, I believe, sold by Messrs. Maignen and Co., and, contrary to most advertised articles, is good.

Together with a plentiful water supply, I may urge the reader to bear in mind how very necessary it is to take all precautions against fire, and to endeavour to secure the means for putting one out, should he have the misfortune to have one break out in his stables, and to see that such arrangements as he may be able to make are ever kept in working order. A few of the hand-grenades sold nowadays should be kept in readiness where they can be instantly got at in case of their being required. They are *really good*, and most thoroughly answer the purpose for which they are intended, and they are moderate in price.

Every stable and its contents should be also fully insured against fire, and the horses against accident, and, I may add, the carriage and harness likewise.

Should a stable be on fire, the first thing is, of course, to endeavour to get the horses out of danger. Now, it is a *most difficult thing* to induce a horse to leave a burning stable—indeed, almost *impossible*—unless they are bridled or have an ordinary driving headstall put on. Strange to say, there is then no difficulty at all. Why this *should* be so, I have never been able to ascertain; but such *is* the case, and I think I may as well state the fact here, while it is in my mind.

CHAPTER VI.

Stable doors.—Carelessness of grooms in leading horses in and out of stables.—Good grooms *v.* bad.

WE have so far considered the external construction of the stable, its walls, roofing, lighting, etc., and it now remains to further decide what is the best kind of doorway to use.

I know nothing better than that in use in the officers' stables in the cavalry barracks at Colchester. It is simplicity itself, and more durable than any other system with which I am acquainted. Each door is divided into two halves horizontally, viz., an upper and lower half. The *lower* portion is slung on hinges in the ordinary way, and is fastened with a bolt and hand-latch of circular form, with a folding-ring handle—this latter being countersunk so as to offer no projections to horses in entering or leaving the stable. The upper half runs on small wheels on a rail on the top of the lower door when it is desirable to close it, and back into the wall, or, I should rather say, into 'rebates' fixed on the inside of the wall. Thus either the top or bottom half of the door may be opened or closed at will ; but when *both* are closed each supports and locks the other.

There is in this arrangement no chance of horses being damaged, no hanging of doors, and the wear and tear is reduced very considerably, and inasmuch as they fit so closely, there is very little, if any, possible draught.

With such doors as these it is, if space permits, quite possible to have doors at either end of even a *small* stable. Their cost may exceed that of the ordinary doors in the first instance ; but in the long-run they would, I am sure, be found economical.

Of course, in a large stable there should be doors at either end, and, where there are a great many horses, doors in the front side as well—say one for every four or five stalls.

Whatever system of door may be adopted, I would urge the reader to set his face *most strongly* against any fastenings which offer any projections either in the way of hasps or handles, for they are the constant cause of damage to horses ; and the edges of all door-posts should be rounded off, so as to, as far as possible, minimize the chance of damage.

Grooms are exceedingly careless in leading

horses through doorways; as often as not they lead the way, dragging the horse after them, and the result may be, and often is, an injury to the horse's hip. Many a horse is set 'down at hip,' as it is termed, from their carelessness in this respect. A *good* groom would, of course, never be guilty of such carelessness; but how many really *good* grooms is one fortunate enough to secure in a lifetime?

It may be thought that I am perhaps very much 'down on' grooms. So I am on the bad and careless, and rightly, too, I consider. They deserve to be blamed, and, what is more, they know it too; no one knows it better. But for a really honest, hard-working groom I have every respect. Grooming is hard and monotonous work: day in, day out, the work is the same, with little or no variety, and with far too often no commendation—nay, barely any notice taken of the results of his labour. The master, perhaps, very rarely visits his stable, although morning after morning it is in spick and span order, and arranged as if his coming were expected. But more of this later on; I am somewhat straying from my subject, and I wish to keep its several details as separate as I possibly can.

CHAPTER VII.

Stable fittings.—Stalls.—Loose-boxes.—Stall partitions.—Government stable fittings.—Wood for partitions.—Racks and mangers.—Feeding on the ground.—Movable fittings.—Fork and broom racks.—Shelves.—Stall-post pegs.—Dust and dirt.—Slovenly servants.

I WILL now proceed to discuss what are termed the internal fittings of the stable. First of all I would draw attention to the fact that the stalls are usually made far too narrow, and horses, therefore, in being turned round in them, are very apt to knock themselves about. They should, on the contrary, be of such a width that a big horse can move round with perfect ease; they are also frequently wanting in depth.

As I remarked before, horses are apt, when the slope of the 'standing' is excessive, to rein back on to the gangway. If the stall is deep enough this should be impossible. Moreover, if they are wide and deep enough, it is an easy matter to contrive a loose-box by putting up bails of wood across from the stall-post to the wall, and this is often a very great convenience; besides which, a good wide stall gives a horse ample room to roll without fear of his getting cast. Again, a shallow stable gives insufficient room for the gangway, and this, in the case of a kicking or vicious horse, is dangerous. Of course, where it can be managed, there is nothing so good as a horse-box; but it is a luxury which is not within the reach of everyone, although a great many of the modern stables are constructed so as to give each horse a box to himself. Where such exist they generally, and, indeed, always, should have the upper part of the partitions railed with iron, so as to allow as free a passage of air through the stable as can be secured. It is argued that boxes consume more straw than stalls. I do not think they do, inasmuch as the straw is not so trampled down and soiled as in a stall. It may take more straw at *first* to litter a box, but if properly attended to, and not carelessly wasted, it will require no more additional daily straw to keep up the requisite supply than a stall; indeed, I doubt very much if the consumption is not actually *less*.

Where stalls are used the partition should be movable. In Government stables, at least in those used for the officers' horses, they are invariably so constructed. The stall-post is of iron, and fits into a slot in an iron plate fixed to the floor and into a groove of wood fixed to the ceiling. From this post to the wall on the manger side of the stable there is a bent iron beading, which is grooved so as to admit the heads of the partition-boards. The tails of the latter are fixed into an iron grooved plate on the floor, running from the stall-post to the wall. The ends of the iron beading are mortised into an upright post fixed against the wall at one end, and the other end drops into a slot cut in the stall-post, and the whole is bolted with a hinged iron plate in the stall-post, which shuts flat into it and fixes the head of the beading. This style of partition is very easily removed and replaced, and the boards, being tongued and grooved, can be taken apart and either cleaned or packed away, as may be required. If either of them get broken by kicking, it can be easily replaced by any ordinary carpenter. These boards should, however, not be made of deal; beech, oak, or pitch-pine are better, and less liable to splinter, and though perhaps rather more expensive at first, are more durable, and consequently more economical in the long-run.

We now come to the consideration of mangers and racks. There is nowadays but one material admissible for these, and that is enamelled iron; but they should be placed on the same level with each other, and should not be fixtures to the wall, but made so as to hang from it by claws and rings, or else by a bolting bar. All mangers, whether of iron or wood, should be kept scrupulously clean, and *constantly* scrubbed out with salt and water.

The old system of placing the hay in a rack *above* the horse was bad. First of all, why should the wretched animal be compelled to crane its neck up in the air each time it wanted a mouthful of hay? Again, the seeds from the hay were constantly falling into the eyes of horses, and caused great pain and inflammation; added to which nature never intended a horse to gather his food up in the air, but to eat it off the ground; nowadays many people discard racks and mangers altogether, and feed their horses entirely on the ground. This is a plan, however, with which I cannot altogether agree, inasmuch as not only much food is wasted in the straw, but it must most certainly tend to encourage a horse to eat his bedding, and that is by no means to be desired, and, moreover, it is hardly possible to give bran mashes on the ground. Where a horse is a gross feeder and bolts his food, it may perhaps be a wise plan; but I should prefer to feed such horses little at a time and more frequently.

Where possible, all stable fittings should be of iron, painted to protect them from rust, and movable. The simpler and fewer the fittings and paraphernalia in a stable, the better. The fewer fittings, the less dust and dirt and the fewer things to keep clean. All forks, brooms, shovels, etc., should be placed, and when not in use *kept*, in racks which are sold for that purpose, and should *never* under any circumstances be left lying about or resting against the wall. A sudden jar may knock a fork down, and it is quite possible that the first person who goes into the stable may, not seeing it, run it into his foot; besides which, it is *untidy*, and untidiness in a stable is inadmissible.

One or two simple shelves are useful in a stable, but not one more than is absolutely necessary. These should be made so as to take down easily, daily if required, and *nothing* but the actual *grooming* utensils be ever allowed on them, and on no account should any cupboards be permitted. Cupboards simply become receptacles for all sorts of rubbish, to say nothing of grog-bottles, etc. A peg whereon to hang the dung-basket completes the list of necessaries, unless it be one long peg of wood or iron, as the case may be (the latter for choice), high up on the stall-posts, for hanging harness, etc., on, when harnessing or unharnessing.

Everything which can possibly harbour one speck of dust or dirt should be kept out of a stable. Dust and dirt should be kept down with a strong hand, remembering that the more articles there are, the more dust; the more dust, the more dirt; the more dirt, the more disease. I cannot speak too strongly on this subject. What *can* be more unsightly in a stable than a row of dusty, dirty bottles, with here and there an old currycomb, a worn-out bandage or two, and perhaps, crammed in between these, the stump of an old tobacco-pipe? And ten to one that a match-box, which is sure to be smothered with lumps of tallow (such match-boxes always *are* smothered with candle-grease), is lying alongside of them, and very probably the fag-end of an old tallow-candle. Where articles such as these are to be seen in a stable, it is needless to expect to see clean or well-conditioned horses; other things will be on a par. The servant is a sloven, and the master is either ignorant or a sloven too—'like master, like man.' Probably the whole establishment, inside and out, partakes of the same character. As far as the *stable* is concerned, I should very much doubt if the master is a sportsman, for if so, he would never be so careless of his stable. It argues to me that the groom is aware that his master either does not *know* or does not care, and so he takes advantage of him. My advice to a master who finds his groom careless or dirty in his stable is to get another as soon as he can, and not to waste time and property after he has duly cautioned him. It *must* come to dismissal sooner or later, and is only a matter of time. Therefore it is well to abridge the intervening period as much as possible, and so save a possibly worse state of things and much vexation. When a servant is careless or untidy, he is not *trying* to do his work (I mean, of course, a servant who is supposed to know his business). His heart is not *in* it. Good service must be willingly given. If it has to be extracted at what may be termed the sword's point, it becomes wellnigh valueless, and the strain on both master and man becomes too great to continue for any length of time, and *must* end in a 'blow up' and parting company. Therefore, the sooner the man conveys himself and his talents to a sphere where they may be more appreciated, the better for both of them.

CHAPTER VIII.

Stable necessaries.—Pillar-reins.—Necessity for looping up pillar-reins.—Accidents from loose pillar-reins.—List of grooming utensils.—List of stable utensils.—Brushes.—Work done by the blind.—Body-brushes.—Water-brushes. — Dandy-brushes. — Curry-combs. — Mane-combs. — Sponges. — Hoof-pickers. — Stable rubbers. — Chamois leathers.—Burnishers.—Saddle-soap.—Clipping machines. —Singeing-lamps.—Stable scissors.—Average prices of grooming utensils. — Stable brooms. — Wheelbarrows. — Buckets.—Stable lamps and lighting.—Candle-ends.— Corn-measures —Corn-sieves.—Corn-bins.—Prices of corn-bins.—Average price of stable utensils.

I THINK I have in the foregoing enumerated all of what may be called the actual fittings of the stable—the fixtures; and I will now proceed to take notice of the smaller articles which are necessary, such as pillar-reins, brooms, forks, shovels, brushes, and the necessary grooming utensils, etc. Pillar-reins are a necessary, and are used to fasten a horse to when he is saddled or harnessed and waiting to go out.

There are various kinds—iron chains, leather straps, and cords. I prefer the latter. They last quite as long as the leather, and, if kept properly pipe-clayed, *look* better. The white, solid, eight-plaited cord is the best cord for the purpose; and these should have a brass spring-hook at either end, by which to attach them to the rings on the stall-posts at one end and the bit at the other. If of leather, they are usually made at one end to buckle and strap on to the post-rings, and with a spring-hook at the other. Chains I do not care for; and they don't look smart, though they wear, practically speaking, for ever. But of whatever material pillar-reins are made, when not in use they should invariably be kept looped up, and *especially* where chains are used.

I have known the most serious consequences occur from neglect of this precaution. Mares, especially when 'horsing,' as it is called, are very apt to rub their quarters against the stall-posts and swish their tails about, and at times to get the pillar-reins *under their tails*, and do themselves really serious injury. It seems, perhaps, incredible that such a thing could easily occur or be more than an isolated instance.

A case of this kind occurred in my own stables some years ago, and I was at a loss to understand how the injury could have been sustained. I had at the time a very handsome, well-bred mare as a first charger. She was always very fidgety in the stable at night, and when 'in season' exceptionally so. One morning my groom reported to me that she had got damaged, and he could not explain how it had happened; but it looked as if someone had maliciously torn her 'bearing' with some sharp instrument. I was naturally much distressed about it, and reported the circumstance to the colonel, who ordered an investigation to be made. I could not suspect my groom, for he had been some time with me, and was invariably gentle to, and fond of, his horses, and I could not for a moment think it possible that I had any enemy capable of doing me such an injury.

My regiment was at this time at Aldershot. Happening to meet Mr. Pallin, then the veterinary surgeon of the 20th Hussars, I told him of the unlucky occurrence. After listening to what I had to say, he said: 'You may make your mind quite easy about it. No one has done it but the mare herself, with the key of the pillar-chains,' adding that it was by no means an uncommon accident. Strange to say, not long after this we had one or two similar cases occur amongst the troop-horses; and from that time all the pillar-chains were ordered to be looped up when not in use.

I mention this fact, since it may not only be interesting to the reader, but may serve to impress upon him the *reason* why pillar-reins should be looped up ; and, as I stated at the commencement of this book, I think it of consequence to give the why and the wherefore, in order that the right way of doing things may be secured and the *wrong* avoided.

The cleaning articles required by a groom are but few in number, but they should be good of their kind. They are as follows :

Body-brush.
Water ditto.
Dandy ditto.
Curry-comb.
Mane ditto.
Two sponges—one large, one small.
Hoof-pick.
Three rubbers.
Two chamois leathers.
Burnisher.
Soap (common yellow).

To these may be added the following, which will do for the use of the stable generally, viz.,

Clipping machine.
Singeing-lamp.
Pair of scissors.

For the use of the *stable itself*, the following are also requisite :

   Birch or whalebone brooms.
   Stable fork.
   Shovel.
   Wheelbarrow.
   Dung-basket.
   Stable lantern.
   Ditto buckets.
   Corn-measures.
   Ditto sieves.

Now, I propose taking all these in the order in which I have enumerated them, and will endeavour to explain, for the use of the reader, how to purchase good articles, giving, as nearly as I can, the average price of each one.

Brushes vary as much in quality as any article well-nigh can. A good brush will wear out at *least two* bad ones, and it is impossible to get a good one at a low price. Firstly, because good bristles are dear, and good work is never cheap. If the reader will take the trouble to examine a good brush, he will see that it is composed of a number of small tufts of bristles, which are doubled through holes in a wooden back, and that the back of the brush is covered over with a thin piece of wood in order to protect the bristle-ends on that side, as also to give it a more finished appearance. In a good brush this backing is generally *screwed* on; in an inferior article it is glued, and here, at once, there is a marked difference, as where the latter may, and will, probably, soon come off, the *former* will, or *should*, remain on as long as the bristles last. Now, if he will again turn the brush over and examine the tufts of bristles, he will see that each bristle is equally good. Let him now take an inferior brush and make a similar inspection, and he will see that in the centre of each tuft the bristles are inferior to those outside the tuft—in fact, that the tufts are adulterated; and so it goes on with those still more inferior, until he will find in the worst kind scarcely any bristles at all, but all rubbish. Some years ago I was talking on the subject of brush-making to a blind lad who was a protégé of my family, and who earned his living by brush-making, and he explained to me that the blind could not adulterate brushes. They could, he said, make brushes of altogether *bad*, or altogether *good* material; but they could not manage to arrange the bad in the centre of the good so as not to be at once apparent. I used to employ him to make my horse-brushes, and some of my brother officers also gave him orders, and very good they were. They were, perhaps, not so elaborately finished and varnished up as those I could have bought at a saddler's for nearly the same price, but the material and work were *excellent*, and they wore to the very last. I would urge my readers, where they can conveniently do so, to purchase their stable brushes, etc., from some of the blind institutions. I believe *all* their work is good and sound. I do not think it is very much cheaper than that performed by other workmen; but it is reliable, and it is a satisfaction to feel that, in addition to obtaining value for one's money, one is also helping those who, being so terribly afflicted, are striving to help themselves.

Body-brushes.—A good body-brush costs from 5s. to 6s. The latter price is ample, though some of the shops will perhaps charge 6s. 6d. for those with polished backs. As the back is just as serviceable whether polished or not, polish is of no consequence, and can be dispensed with.

Water-brush.—What I have remarked as being necessary in a body-brush applies equally to a water-brush. Of course, it is a *sine quâ non* that, the brush being constantly wet, the back should be well screwed on and carefully closed. The price of a good water-brush is from 5s. 6d. to 6s., much about the same as a body-brush.

Dandy-brush.—Dandy-brushes are used for brushing off the rough dirt. These are made of whalebone, or whalebone and what is termed whisk. Their price is about 2s. to 2s. 6d.

Curry-combs.—A curry-comb is used for cleaning the body-brush when grooming, and to clear it of the scurf which accumulates on the brush. It should be used for that purpose *alone*, and *not*, as I have seen ignorant grooms do, for scraping the horse with. Could ignorance, and I may almost add brutality, go further than to scrape the skin of a horse with a curry-comb?—which latter, being made of iron and having its edges serrated, must be about as pleasant to the wretched animal as it would be if rubbed with a row of saws. No wonder so many horses are bad to groom. Curry-combs are very inexpensive, and can be bought from 6d. to 1s. each. Those with a webbing handstrap are better than those with handles, being more convenient to hold, and the handles invariably come off after a few days' use.

Mane-combs.—I need not say anything about mane-combs further than that they should be made of horn. *These*, and *not* what are termed, and aptly so, 'mane-drags,' should be used. The latter are useless in a gentleman's stable, and, in the hands of any but the most experienced in their use, are brutally cruel instruments. Mane-combs cost but a very few pence.

Sponges.—Sponges are amongst the more expensive items in the list of stable gear; that is to say, they are made so by servants, but should *not* be. A groom requires two, one large and one small. Now, saddlers never keep cheap sponges, and it is difficult to get a fair-sized sponge at a saddler's under 6s. or 7s. They assure you they are of the best quality, and they doubtless are so; and they assert that, being so, they will last out two or three of a cheaper kind; so they *should*. My experience, however, goes to prove that they do *not*—not from any fault of the sponge itself, but rather through the carelessness of the user. The temptation of a new sponge is too great for some servants, who quietly appropriate them to their own use, and if they do not, they are so careless in wringing them out that they invariably tear them, and all that they have to produce within a short time of what was vaunted to last so long is a torn, wretched strip of a thing. I myself always now buy the cheaper kinds, and I find that a sponge for which I give 1s. or 1s. 6d. lasts just as long as a more expensive one. I therefore recommend the reader to follow my advice. Otherwise he would have more satisfaction if he were to give the extra 5s. to the first beggar he meets, or even to throw it over the hedge where *somebody might* benefit by it.

Hoof-pickers.—Hoof-pickers are necessary evils, and are used for picking out the dung, etc., which may have collected in the horse's feet when standing in the stable. Careless servants are apt to be far too rough in using them, and to pick away with them to the detriment of the horse's feet. They are made of iron, and are very inexpensive—about 2d. each. They should be blunt-pointed, for the reason I have stated above.

Stable Rubbers.—Stable rubbers are cloths made of strong linen; a groom requires about three of them. It is a wise plan to have them marked with the owner's name in ink in large letters and *numbered*. They are less likely to get lost, and the word 'stable' should also be written on them. They should also be provided with a tape loop to hang them up by. Grooms should be expected to wash these and such-like articles *themselves*, and they should not be allowed to form part of the household linen in the weekly wash. When they *do* so, they are soon lost, and, of course, nobody knows anything about them. Their price is about 5s. per dozen.

Chamois Leathers.—Two chamois leathers are sufficient for each groom. In purchasing them, hold them up to the light, in order to detect any thin spots. A small one, uniformly thick, will last longer than a larger one with thin patches. When not in use, those which are wet should be hung carefully to dry, but *not* on a nail or any sharp projection. Good ones cost about 2s. each, and that is a fair average price to give for them.

Burnishers.—It is impossible for a groom to keep the steel-work under his charge bright and properly clean without a burnisher. It should be sewn on to a square of leather which is strong and pliant. Buff is generally used for the purpose. In purchasing a burnisher, do not grudge the price for one of good size. They are somewhat expensive, and cost from about 2s. 6d. to 3s. 6d.

Saddle-soap.—The soap used for saddlery and for stable purposes must be pure and *light-coloured*. The dark-coloured soap, or soft soap, discolours the leather. Saddle-soap can be purchased in round tins, convenient for using, from any saddler for 1s. each, or the plain, old-fashioned yellow soap, such as is used for household purposes, is equally good; indeed, for saddles, etc., I almost prefer it to any other. Soft soap is all very well for washing the white heels of horses, etc., but it should never be used for saddlery or any fine leather.

Each groom should be provided with the abovenamed articles. Those which I have described as useful for the stable generally, would suffice for every three or four horses, and I will take them in the order I have named them :

Clipping Machines.—Clipping machines cost about 7s. 6d. to 10s. 6d. Clark's are as good as any, price 8s. 6d. They require to be kept carefully oiled and clean, and when not in use should be protected with a leather case. The teeth are very apt to get broken with careless usage, and from being thrown down, etc.

Singeing-lamps.—There are two or three kinds of singeing-lamps. The two most generally in use are gas and naphtha. Those for gas are expensive, the latter very *inexpensive*, costing only a shilling or two, as compared with half a guinea or thereabouts. To my way of thinking there is no comparison between the two, and in this instance the cheaper has the advantage. It is true that naphtha-lamps require to be carefully and constantly trimmed; but a good hand will make better work with them, for the flame from gas is too fierce and strong for singeing horses, and is apt to burn them. The naphtha is slower and better altogether, and burns the hair off more regularly.

Stable Scissors.—A pair of stable scissors will be found necessary, and with these there is nothing further required.

The cost of the above-named articles is as follows, viz. :

		£	s.	d.
1 body-brush, say	. .	0	6	6
1 water ditto	. . .	0	5	6
1 dandy ditto	. . . .	0	2	0
1 curry-comb	. . . .	0	0	6
1 mane ditto	. . .	0	0	6
2 sponges, one at 2s. and one at 1s.	.	0	3	0
1 hoof-pick	. . . . .	0	0	6
3 rubbers	. . . . .	0	1	6
2 chamois leathers	. . .	0	4	0
1 burnisher	. . . .	0	3	6
1 clipping machine	. . .	0	8	6
1 singeing-lamp	. . . .	0	2	6
1 pair of stable scissors	. .	0	2	0
		£2	0	6

For the use of the stable itself, the list I have given under the head of 'Stable Requisites' will suffice.

Forks.—Stable forks are often made far too sharp. They are, when so, dangerous, and especially so in the hands of a careless groom. They should be blunt-pointed, and not too long in the handle. They cost about 3s.

Brooms.—Bass-brooms are the best for stable use, as they penetrate every crevice, and wear well. Their price is about 2s.

Birch-brooms.—Birch-brooms answer well enough for the rougher, outside work, and cost about 3s. per dozen.

Shovel.—A stable shovel is also a necessity. Price 3s. 6d.

Wheelbarrow.—A wheelbarrow costs from 15s. to £1.

Dung-basket.—A dung-basket costs from 2s. 6d. to 3s. 6d.

Wooden Buckets.—Wooden buckets are best for stable purposes, and when painted cost about 5s. each.

Iron Pails. — Those of galvanized iron last longer and are less expensive. One wooden one for each horse, and one iron one to every two or three horses, are sufficient. The galvanized iron ones cost about 3s. There is also another description of bucket which is useful for fomentations, etc., if required. It is longer and deeper than the ordinary wooden bucket. These are made of wood.

Stable Lamps and Lighting.—The best light for a stable is undoubtedly gas, but where this is not available, recourse must be had to some other description of light. Side-wall lights, perhaps, give the best light, but they should never be used off the wall, and should be carefully attended to, as the dust from the bedding, etc., very soon accumulates on them. One or two lanterns of the kind known as 'hurricane lanterns' are as good as anything, and these should be slung from the ceiling, so as to be out of the way, and to lessen the chance of their setting fire to anything. They usually burn oil, or some kind of paraffin. I do not like paraffin in a stable, but it gives a good light. A candle lantern is insufficient for the dark winter mornings and evenings, and grooms are so apt to take out the candles and to stick them on the window-sills or anywhere they can. I need hardly caution the reader to be most severely 'down on' anything of the kind. Such malpractices generally leave their traces behind them in the shape of spots of grease and burnt patches of woodwork. A good pattern of 'hurricane stable lamp' is to be obtained at any of the principal shops where such things are sold, for, I think, about 5s.

Corn-measure.—A corn-measure may also be added to the above list; the usual price for a half-gallon one is 1s. (or rather less).

Corn-sieve.—A corn-sieve is useful for sifting the dust from the oats, and also for carrying chaff, etc. The price of them is about 2s.

Corn-bins.—I had intended to make mention of corn-bins later on, but the present is perhaps not inopportune, so I will do so now. I recommend the use of those made of galvanized iron, as being well-nigh imperishable, and rat and mouse proof. The cost of them, which in this instance I have taken from the Army and Navy Co-operative Society's price-list, I append:

	£	s.	d.
To hold 1 sack of corn, from	0	18	0
,, 2 sacks ,, ,,	1	7	9
,, 3 ,, ,, ,,	1	18	6
,, 4 ,, ,, ,,	2	11	9

I should advise the use of one to hold two sacks (for corn), and one to hold one sack (for bran). A third may be found useful for chaff, but it is not necessary. Two of the size I have named would be large enough for a stable of two or three horses. Where practicable, I do not advise that the corn-bins should be kept in the stables, inasmuch as I am so strongly opposed to anything further than the horses and what is *absolutely necessary* being there, greater cleanliness and less lodgment for dust and dirt being thereby secured.

The cost of utensils necessary for a stable of one or two horses will be, therefore, as follows, viz.:

	£	s.	d.
1 stable fork	0	3	0
1 bass-broom	0	2	0
3 birch-brooms	0	0	9
1 wheelbarrow	1	0	0
1 shovel	0	3	6
1 dung-basket	0	3	6
1 wooden bucket	0	5	0
1 iron pail	0	3	0
1 stable lamp	0	5	0
1 half-gallon corn-measure	0	1	0
1 corn-sieve	0	2	0
1 iron corn-bin	1	7	9
1 ,, ,,	0	18	0
	£4	14	6

Nor do I see that this sum can be reduced. The corn-bins, of course, take up half, and the wheelbarrow a quarter, or nearly so, of the sum total; but these are articles which will not require renewing for a long time, especially the former.

CHAPTER IX.

Horse-clothing and horses' coats.—Kerseymere clothing.—
Colour of clothing.—Making up of clothing.—London and
provincial work.—Quarter-sheet and breast-piece.—Fillet-
strings.—Pad and roller.—Improper girthing up of rollers.
—Evils of girthing up of rollers.—Hoods.—Short hoods.
—Fawn striped rugs.—Weight and price of ditto.—How
to test woollen goods.—Night-rugs.—Summer clothing.

THE amount of clothing required for a horse must of course be determined by weather. In this climate there are but few months—I may say but few weeks—in the year during which it is possible to dispense with clothing of some kind.

Horses in stables are compelled to lead a somewhat artificial kind of existence. Naturally speaking, their coats are equal to the occasion, provided they have a sufficient shelter and litter for the nights and more inclement periods of the year; and as a rule, if left alone, their coats, if they are healthy, will generally 'thicken' and 'thin'— 'rise' and 'fall,' as it is termed—according as the weather may be cold or mild; and at these times the very moving of the coat is productive of a considerable amount of scurf, which—coupled with the fact that Providence has seen also fit to arrange that when they most require additional covering their skin, which is always more or less greasy, should become more so—renders them during the colder months of the year more difficult to groom. To facilitate their grooming, as also to save their being exhausted by having to do fast work when burdened with a heavy coat, to prevent possible chills when kept standing after sweating immoderately, as under such circumstances must undoubtedly be the case, we are compelled to remove this natural covering of hair, this winter coat, by means of the clipping machine and singeing-lamp.

It is true that there are some horses which, apparently, never get a winter coat, and whose coats are, to look at, much the same at all seasons of the year; but such are the exceptions to the general rule, and to these we will not here refer.

Having removed this coat for the purpose of work, it is clearly necessary that we must provide the animal, when he is not actually doing work, with a substitute for that which Nature gave him and we have removed.

Horse-clothing, therefore, becomes necessary.

Most horses require during the twenty-four hours from one to three rugs, according to the temperature of the weather.

It will be sufficient to state here that three *good* rugs should be sufficient, as a general rule, for a horse, even in the cold winter nights. If these are really good and of proper weight, *more* than this number is (except under extraordinary circumstances) apt to be weakening.

A full suit of clothing consists of the following, viz. :

A quarter-sheet, hood, pad, roller, and fillet-strings. *One* of these full suits is sufficient for each horse, and is, as a rule, worn only during the daytime, or when the horse is being led at exercise in the winter. The hood is seldom required except in the *very* severest weather, or when travelling by rail, standing at a forge, etc.

This full suit is generally made of kerseymere, which is sold of various patterns, and bound with some coloured cloth—or of plain fawn-coloured kerseymere, bound with blue, red, yellow, etc.

The *colour* is immaterial, provided the *material* is *good*. If there is one colour which I have found wear better and look smarter than any other, it is what is known as the 'Oxford check,' and its having but little dye in it may, perhaps, be the reason of its lasting qualities, as it is, of course, well known that all dyes are more or less apt to rot the material dyed.

However, the colour must depend on the reader's choice. Any saddler will show him a number of good patterns which he can select from; but whatever may be his choice, it is of consequence that the clothing should be properly cut. If *any* saddler were asked if he could make a suit of horse-clothing, he would at once reply 'that he could, of course.' So, likewise, any tailor will assure a customer that he can make a pair of hunting-breeches. The result of believing in this assurance would, I think, go far to prove that the former would probably end in as great a failure as the latter. My own experience reminds me of the most remarkable productions regarding both.

It is *quite the exception* to get horse-clothing well cut. A *good* London or really *first-class* provincial saddler will doubtless be able to do so. The ordinary local man will very possibly provide precisely the same material as the London man, but he either will not or cannot cut it; he either skimps or bags it. It is tight where it should be loose, and *vice versâ*, and short where it should be long, etc. The result is that it is wretchedly uncomfortable to the poor horse, is always getting displaced, and probably causes a sore wither, or, at least, rubs a bare spot on the shoulder points, added to which it looks *beastly* and unsportsmanlike. Yet, if the prices of the two men are compared, the difference will not be found to be so very great ; while for *wearing* qualities, of course the former has immeasurably the best of it, because, *fitting* the horse properly as it does, there is no undue strain upon any one part of it. Of course, there are provincial saddlers who *can* cut a quarter-sheet properly, but they are by no means numerous.

A quarter-sheet is most frequently made in one piece to buckle round in front of the horse's chest ; but it is a better plan to have a *separate* breast-piece—it is warmer, and is not so apt to wear out either the horse or itself. *All* rugs have a tendency to work back, and this being so, the reason why a breast-piece is more advantageous is obvious. Horses very often get severely cut and galled in the withers from a quarter-sheet being improperly made, and such sores take some time in healing.

Fillet-strings are usually made of braid of the same colours as those in the clothing, and are plaited in a hollow round plait. They are fastened to loops on the quarter-sheet, and are used for the purpose of keeping the latter down in its place when out in wind, etc. When in the stable, they are looped up in the centre on to the centre seam of the quarter-sheet, to preserve them from being soiled.

The pad, as it is called, is merely an oblong piece of kerseymere of the same colour as the rest of the clothing, and bound in the same way. It is used to protect the quarter-sheet, as well as the horse's back, from any undue wear from the *roller*, which is a description of girth with a padded back and sides, which is fastened round the horse for the purpose of securing the quarter-sheet in its place. In girthing up the roller, care should be taken that the quarter-sheet is first put on *fairly* and *truly* and *well* forward, with the seam straight down the centre of the horse's back—and this should always be done before the roller is put on—and that it (the roller) is not buckled *too* tightly, and yet tightly enough. If the former is the case the horse must suffer, and all sorts of evils arise from rollers being habitually put on too tight. If not tight enough, the clothing works back or falls round, and, besides leaving the horse without any covering over its loins, and just where covering is *most* necessary, it also is sure to get torn and soiled from being trampled upon; and it is also *quite* possible that a horse may get cast and seriously injured by it.

I have already described the *use* of a hood, so need not repeat it. A hood should fit well and neatly, and be long enough to allow a horse to put his head down without fear of its falling forward. It should be provided with a small buckle and strap wherewith to fasten it, and prevent its blowing over the horse's head in wind. This strap should go through a leather loop sewn on to the wither of the quarter-sheet. Nothing can well be more dangerous than a loose hood flying over a horse's head. I leave the reader to imagine the result of such in the case of a nervous horse. To avoid the chance of this, *short* hoods are sometimes used. They are sufficient protections to the head and throat, but of course are not quite so effective a covering as the ordinary hood.

The foregoing remarks on horse-clothing *suits* comprise all the details which I consider worthy of notice—at all events, all which is necessary for the present occasion.

The price of a full suit of kerseymere varies, of course, as to the *quality* of the material; but a good suit should not cost more than between four or five guineas, and should, with ordinary care, last some years.

For what may be called intermediate clothing, the ordinary fawn striped rugs, weighing from 8 lb. to 9 lb., can be used instead of the more expensive clothing; and these can, if desired, be cut out and bound in the same manner as the kerseymere quarter-sheet, or can be used plain, as sold; but they should be guaranteed to be *all wool*. The heavier they are, of course, the better. They are sold by weight, at the uniform price of 2s. per lb. weight, and when purchasing them I would advise the reader to always see them weighed. And here I may as well take the opportunity of remarking that if, when purchasing any goods which are guaranteed to be 'all wool,' he has any doubts as to their being so, he can very easily satisfy himself as to whether such is the case or not if he draws a thread from both the warp and the woof of the material and picks them to pieces. If there is any admixture of cotton or other such inferior substance, it will, on being held up to the light, be at once apparent, and he will, of course, do well to reject it, as such material can never be warm, or wear satisfactorily. It is well to know this, and I have many a time been saved buying a worthless article by taking the trouble to thus examine it.

There is another very good kind of rug, which is

composed of strong canvas waterproofed and lined with rugging, which is most useful as a night-rug, to put over the other rugs, and to prevent their being soiled. The roller, which should be made of leather, is sewn on to it. When soiled, these rugs are easily cleaned with soap and water, but the water should not be warm. They should be made *full large*, so as to allow for the other rugs beneath. The price of them is, for the best quality, and of the pattern I have described, about 17s. 6d. for the full size.

There are several cheaper varieties of these rugs, but they are very common, do not wear well, and have but little real warmth in them. The best I ever had I bought from Mr. Stone, the saddler at Aldershot, for autumn manœuvres. I do not know if he still supplies them, but have no doubt that he does; and here I may mention that I wish the reader to distinctly understand that, where in the present little work I may have occasion to make mention of the name of any tradesman or firm, I do so solely for his (the reader's) benefit, and not, as is so often the fashion nowadays, as an advertisement for the tradesman. Such is entirely contrary to my wish or intention.

Summer clothing is clothing made of linen, and is generally made in the entire suit, similar to the kerseymere suits. It is useful to keep off flies, dust, etc., and looks smart and clean. As a rule, a quarter-sheet, pad or roller, and fillet-strings are sufficient *without* the hood. Its price is about £2 10s.

CHAPTER X.

Bandages. — Mode of tying bandages. — Cracked heels. — Woollen bandages.—Hunting bandages.—Support from bandages. — Colour of material for bandages. — Care of bandages. — 'Naphthaline' for prevention of moth in woollen goods, etc.—'Naphthaline' for saddles.—Stocking bandages.—Water bandages.—Chamois-leather bandages. —Sweating bandages.—Bandaging.—Prices of bandages.

BANDAGES are made of several kinds of material, viz., woollen, linen, stocking, and chamois leather; but of whatever description they may be, they require to be very carefully put on, care being taken not to fit them *too* tightly, as each fold tightens the previous one.

They are, generally speaking, tied a few inches below the knee, or else about the centre of the leg. This is wrong. They should be tied low down on the fetlock joint. They do not, perhaps, look as well, but it is the best place, for if a bandage is put on ever so loosely, there must be always a certain amount of pressure, and if too great pressure is had in the broad fold of the bandage itself, it must be still worse in the narrow fold of the tape. The joint, therefore, seems to me to be the best and proper place for the tape to be tied, being less susceptible of pressure than the tendons.

This method of tying bandages was shown me many years ago by a friend whose opinion on such matters is worth having. It is, however, but rarely that one sees it adopted. It is no easy matter to put on a bandage properly and neatly, and requires care and practice.

After exercise, woollen bandages should always be put on for a time, and should be rolled well into the hollow of the heel, thus serving to absorb any sweat, as well as any damp, which may remain if the legs are wet or have been washed, which latter, by-the-bye, they never *should* be.

Horses' heels are more or less damp after exercise, and sweat very readily runs into the hollows and collects there, and is liable, if left to dry itself, to cause cracked heels, which are difficult and troublesome to cure.

I do not, of course, wish it to be supposed that bandaging should take the place of drying by hand, but only as an additional precaution against cracked heels. Some horses are very predisposed to cracked heels, but thoroughbred horses are, perhaps, less liable to get them than underbred animals.

Woollen bandages, properly put on, are also the next best thing to hand-rubbing, though, of course, they are vastly inferior to it. The one should follow the other.

Such bandages are invaluable for old horses, and horses whose legs are 'filled' from overwork, and are a great support to their legs, and in winter they are warm. In some rough hunting countries they are much used as a protection to horses' legs against stone walls, etc. ; but when they are used for this, or any similar purpose, they require to be very carefully put on and tied ; indeed, they are almost better if stitched on, as they are otherwise apt to come undone, and very likely at the time when hounds are running, and the necessity of having to dismount and readjust them may possibly be the cause of losing a good place in a good run. Indeed, the only thing to do under such circumstances is to pull off the bandage altogether. I have myself, on more than one occasion, experienced this annoyance, and invariably have a few stitches put into the folds here and there as they are laid.

Horses which have not got the advantage of a loose-box require the support and pressure of bandages if their legs are at all apt to 'fill.' There are some horses whose legs *never* 'fill,' even with the *severest* work. I believe that, except for drying and warming purposes, it is better *not* to bandage the legs of such horses in the stable, and that their legs are kept tougher without them.

Woollen bandages are sold of different colours. Experience has taught me that the fawn-coloured and white last longest. Saddlers have assured me that the *material* is the same, no matter what the *colour* may be. I can but conclude, therefore, that the colour of the dye affects the material. The white ones soon get dirty and discoloured, and require to be constantly washed, and so wear out sooner than they otherwise would.

When not in use, *all* bandages should be kept neatly rolled up, and should be well dried and brushed before being put away. Brushing is better than washing, as the latter is apt to shrink them. All spare bandages, and everything of a woollen nature which is used for stable purposes, should be constantly overhauled and exposed to the air and sun, in order to prevent the ravages of moths; and here I may as well advise the reader to keep a small quantity of what is called 'naphthaline' in the saddle-room. It is a white powder in a crystallized form, very cleanly, and requires to be but placed (a very small quantity will suffice) in a tray on the saddle-room shelves, or hanging it up in small muslin bags will suffice for the purpose. It has a rather pungent, but not altogether disagreeable, smell, and no moth will come near it. It does not scent the articles themselves, and there is *nothing* equally efficacious for the purpose.

As is well known, saddles, if uncared for, are *sure* to become a prey to moth, and I would advise that a small quantity of this powder should be mixed up with the horsehair stuffing under the pannels of each saddle. No matter how much a saddle may suffer from neglect in other ways, it will not be attacked by moth if this is done.

I may add that 'naphthaline' is most useful for other things, such as furs, feathers, etc., and immeasurably superior to the moth-powders usually sold, and which do *not* secure complete immunity from moth, and seem to lose their virtue after a short time. It can be procured from any good chemist for a few pence an ounce, and the latter quantity will go a long way and last a long time.

Stocking bandages are woven hollow in the same manner as stockings, and are made of some sort of fine wool or cotton, or mixture of both. They are used principally for racing purposes, and are somewhat expensive.

Water bandages are made entirely of linen; the best are those which are made of twilled linen. They are, as their name implies, used *wet*, for the purpose of reducing inflammation, etc.

The twilled linen retains the water longer than the finer material. When water bandages are used, they must be kept constantly wetted, as if they are allowed to get dry they are worse than no bandages at *all*. When new they should always be well soaked for some hours. In every case before applying a wet bandage to a horse's leg, it is advisable to rub a little grease (oil or glycerine) into the hollow of the heel before the bandage is applied, in order to prevent the heel becoming cracked; and this should be done whether the bandage is wetted with water only or with any kind of lotion. The *best* kind of bandage to use as a *wet* bandage is one made of chamois leather. These remain wet for a very long time, but they are somewhat expensive, and do not last long. They are, however, far superior to a linen bandage. There is a description of bandage which is a combination of a wet and woollen, called a sweating bandage, which has a very powerful effect in reducing swellings, etc. It is, in fact, what doctors call a wet compress, and is formed by putting on first a wet—linen or chamois leather—bandage; then enveloping this with either a piece of oiled silk or waterproof, and over all a dry woollen bandage. Such bandages should not, however, be used for too many days consecutively, but should, as a rule, be three days on and two days off.

It must be borne in mind that whereas, in the *ordinary* way of putting on a bandage, it is usual to commence from the top and finish at the top on the return folds, and tie either there or in the middle of the leg, in putting them on in the manner I have described, it must be commenced from the bottom and finished there, thus bringing the tie to the fetlock-joint, the tie being, of course, on the *outside* of the leg.

The prices of bandages are as follows :

	s.	d.
Woollen (per set of 4) . . .	5	6
Linen (per set of 4), twill . .	5	0

CHAPTER XI.

Stable headstalls.—Prices of headstalls.—Lead-lines.—Logs. — Fitting of lead-lines. — Prices of lead-lines. — Prices quoted for articles.—Good and bad articles.—Rack-chains.—Spring-hooks.—New patent hooks—Kneecaps.—Use of kneecaps. — Evils of kneecaps. — Proper description of kneecaps.—Kneecaps too tightly fitted.—How to fit on kneecaps.—Necessity for obtaining good articles.—Price of kneecaps.—Watering bridles.—Watering snaffles.—Dirty watering snaffles.—Reins for watering snaffles.—Care and condition of watering snaffles.—Accidents from rotten reins.—Mode of fitting watering-bridle reins.—Leading-reins. — Useful maxims. — Exercising without saddles.—Price of watering bridles.

STABLE headstalls should be made of broad, strong leather and double-stitched. Both throat-lash and nose-band should fit loosely, and the former should be round, so as to allow the play of the metal ring which is attached to the leather billet which connects them. This metal ring is for the purpose of securing the lead-line to the headstall, the spring-hook or buckle and strap (as the case may be) of the former being fastened to it.

Brass mountings look better than any other, and

set off a horse's head better. The brow-band may with advantage be made of white buff leather; this, if kept pipe-clayed, looks very clean and smart. Brow-bands of white enamelled leather do not answer, as they are not strong, and the enamel soon cracks and looks shabby. Stable headstalls should be carefully cut so as to fit easily and well, otherwise they are very apt to cause head-sores. Some horses have a habit of slipping their headstalls. Where such is the case they must be buckled on more tightly; but such horses are better in loose-boxes, where the latter are available. I may as well here remark that *coloured* brow-bands are *nowhere* admissible, and white only for stable use. Of course I do not refer to metal *harness* brow-bands.

The prices of stable headstalls vary from about 5s. to 10s., according to quality; 7s. 6d. is a good medium price.

Lead-lines are of leather, chain, or of ordinary rope. Personally, I prefer those made of all chain. Exception may be taken to the noise they make as the horse moves them up and down in the manger-rings, but as they are in general use in the cavalry, I have got so used to them that I do not dislike them. They wear for ever, and horses do not chew at them, as they are so apt to do with leather ones. Rope lines are the worst of all, as they soon fray, and are untrustworthy. Apart from their inducement for horses to play with them, the leather ones do not last very long, and require more care than is usually given to such articles. Where they or rope are used, the log is usually made of wood, but for chain ones an iron log is necessary—at all events is best; and the last link of the chain is fitted with a flat piece of iron called a 'key,' and this is made so as to turn up into the last link. The iron log is pierced through with a hole, which is extended into a cross of equal length each way. The key and last link are passed through this open space, and as the key falls open out of the link it thus secures the log. The whole thing has the appearance of a Russian puzzle, but it is very simple and effective. As in everything else, so there is a right and wrong way to fit such an apparently simple arrangement as a lead-line. It must be a certain length, no more and no less. If too short, the horse cannot lie down; if too long, it is dangerous and apt to cast him. The way to ascertain the right length is thus: Lead the horse up to the manger until his throat is over the manger-ring, his head being held naturally as he stands thus. The log at the end of the lead-line should rest fairly on the ground, and no more.

That will give the proper length for the lead-line, which, if a chain, can be shortened by passing the spring-hook down to the proper link in the chain; if of leather, by knotting up the leather below the log; if of rope, the knot should be what is called a 'blood knot,' the end of the rope being doubled through the loop of the knot, so as to allow of its being quickly and easily untied if required.

Where it is of leather and chain (which, next to chain, is perhaps the best description of lead-line) it can be shortened by the buckle and strap at the head end. The prices of lead-lines are as follows: Leather and chain, about 4s. 6d.; logs (*lignum vitæ*), 1s.

I may as well inform the reader that in giving the prices of any articles I do not give the *very* highest, but I have endeavoured to give what he can rely on obtaining a really good, well-finished article for at a really high-class London saddler's. He can of course please himself as to where he deals, and could, I know, obtain them very much cheaper than at the cost I have reckoned them to be; but I always prefer to get a second-quality article from a really good maker rather than one which an inferior maker would recommend as his best quality, for the simple reason that the prices are probably much the same; and although you *may* get a good article from a second-rate shop, you will never get a bad one from a really first-rate one, and the 'cut' is far superior, and being so, the article in question *must* last longer and look better.

Rack-chains are chains fixed to the stable-wall above the mangers to staples driven in, and are used to prevent horses from lying down and rolling during the daytime. These are generally reckoned as stable fixtures. They cost about 2s. each. Where they are *not* fixtures, it is a wise plan to have spring-hooks at *each* end of the chain; but such hooks should be, as should *all* spring-hooks for stable purposes, strong and well made.

There is a new pattern of *double hook* which I lately saw, and which was procured from Messrs. Holtzappfel and Co., in Cockspur Street, which struck me as being the best thing of the kind as yet invented, and which would quite supersede the spring-hook in general use, and which, having no spring, could not get out of order. It is *very* simple, but requires to be seen to be explained. It is made in all sizes, and in different kinds of metal. I saw one small enough for a watch-chain, made of steel, and some, large enough for any stable purposes, of galvanized iron. I need not add that they were very well finished, but I may remark that they were *excessively moderate* in price. I cannot now remember the name of the patentee, but the reader can, if he wishes, obtain them at Messrs. Holtzappfel's. I *think*, if I remember aright, that the price of the galvanized iron ones is 1s. each. A spring-hook of the same material would cost perhaps a little *less*, but certainly would wear only half the time of the others.

Knee-caps are what may be called necessary evils. They are necessary to prevent horses banging their knees about when travelling by train, etc. They are also commonly used for exercising purposes. It is at such times, when they are ridden by grooms, that the majority of accidents occur. A careless groom—and such servants are, generally speaking, bad horsemen—will sooner or later bring down the best-actioned horse in the world. For exercising purposes, therefore, they are useful; but I myself prefer to dispense with them when I know my servants to be careful and trustworthy, inasmuch as, although it is true that they may save a horse's knees from being blemished, if that horse has the misfortune to fall, I consider that they are in themselves frequently the cause of their falling, especially if of a bad shape.

It is well to here consider what the shape of a kneecap ought to be. Very frequently they are made with nothing further than a round leather cap, which is sewn on to a piece of horsecloth or some such material. Now, if the shape of a horse's knee is examined, it will be observed that it is not round, but oval; and when the knee is bent up in action, it very materially increases in size. It is therefore necessary that the cap of the kneecap should be sufficiently large to allow of the perfectly free and unrestrained movement of the knee, and without strain on the straps which fasten it on above. If this is not the case, as may be readily inferred, the horse's action must either be impeded or the strap of the kneecap must give and burst. If the former, the horse, being unable to bend his knee properly, may, in consequence, fall; if the latter, the kneecap becomes a useless encumbrance.

A kneecap, therefore, requires to be made scientifically. The upper strap, or stay, is that one of the two which kneecaps are provided with, and which serves to keep the latter *up;* the lower strap is intended to keep it *down.* It is therefore obvious that the upper strap must be tight enough for the purpose, and yet, if too tight, it will either burst or cut into the flesh. It is no uncommon thing to see a white ring of hair above and below the knees of a horse. These indicate that at some time some fool of a groom has buckled the kneecaps on too tightly, and that they have cut into the leg. In order to prevent this, in a great measure, the best description of kneecaps are provided with short bands of indiarubber, which give with the expansion of the leg-muscles when in action. The lower strap should be fitted on loosely enough to allow of the breadth of two fingers between it and the leg.

The reader will, from the above and other explanations which I have given, see how very necessary it is to know *why* and *wherefore* articles should, or should not, be of this or that description, and that there is a reason, and a good one too, for their adoption or rejection. People who are uninformed on these matters may probably go to a shop, purchase an article, and hand it over to their servants for use, believing that they have done the best they can regarding its selection; yet all the time they are but setting a trap, as it were, to catch an accident, or cause an evil worse than the very one which they seek to prevent, and all for the want of a little knowledge.

A good horse is a treasure, to be preserved in health as long as possible; he has probably, too, cost a large sum of money; yet, for the sake perhaps of only an extra shilling or two, or a little extra trouble in the purchase and selection of the articles required for his use, etc., he may be ruined in a minute. How often, alas, is such the case! 'The eye of the master is the best servant,' when that master has the full use of his sight and knows about what he sees. The price of a good pair of kneecaps is about 6s. to 7s. 6d. But one more article remains to be treated of in the present chapter, viz., the watering bridle, or exercise bridle, as it is sometimes called.

As a rule, *anything* is considered good enough for an exercising bridle. Now, as a majority of the accidents which happen to horses occur when they are at exercise (and in the stable), it is surely at variance with common-sense to incur any further risk of accident through the use of an inferior article. I make bold enough to assert that one half of the exercising bridles in use are downright rotten. The snaffles are generally made of galvanized iron, or covered with rust, and probably a coating of half-masticated food, showing that from time to time the horse has been pulled away from his feed before he has finished it, in order to suit the groom's convenience, or because, he having been late that morning, the feed has been hurried and the exercise-hour also hurried on. Of course, under good management such a state of things would not exist; but, let me ask, how often is such the case?

A watering-bridle snaffle of this description is truly a nice thing to put into a horse's mouth, especially when the metal casing with which such snaffles are covered is flaking off, and the surface is consequently rough. It is difficult at any time to find a groom with what are called 'hands.' What, then, must be the effect of such an instrument in the mutton-fisted grasp of one without 'hands,' on a horse whose mouth is delicate and tender? No; galvanized iron is a very useful thing in its *proper place*, but that place is *not* in the mouth of a *horse*.

Again, the reins of exercising bridles are often made of cheap, common leather, instead of good, sound material; and they are very constantly *buckled* on to the snaffle, thereby, inasmuch as there is ever so much more stitching to rot and get out of order, wearing out much sooner than they would if sewn on to the rings.

I maintain that exercising bridles should be kept as clean as those for the use of the master, and a good groom will take care that they are so.

We will suppose that the ordinary description of uncared-for bridle is in use on a horse. It is perhaps a chilly morning, and the horse is a bit fresh. Something startles him, and he tries to bolt. The groom pulls at him—most probably the *pull* is a severe 'job' in the mouth; bang goes the rotten leather, and away goes the horse; the groom gets pitched off, and possibly badly hurt; and the horse, after half killing a few people, tries to kill himself, and not unfrequently succeeds in doing so.

Both ends of the reins of an exercising bridle should be sewn on to the snaffle-rings, and *not*, as is sometimes the case, only *one* end sewn on, and the other with an iron key to slip through and hold across the other ring. Such an arrangement is only fit for a leading-rein.

When it is required to lead a horse with a snaffle-bridle, throw the reins over his head and pass a rein through the snaffle-ring its entire length under the jaw of the horse, on whichever side it may be wished to lead from.

If it is desired to lead a horse at any time with an ordinary double rein (bit and bridoon), do so in the following way: Lay each rein in its order on the horse's neck; the snaffle will then, of course, be that nearest the head. Now lift up the bit-rein and pass it over the snaffle-rein, and let it lie there. Again lift up the *snaffle*-rein, and, passing it over the bit-rein, carry it over the horse's head; it will then hang down from the snaffle-rings *between* the bit-reins (the latter are still left on the horse's neck). Now pass the snaffle-rein through the ring of the snaffle as described for a single snaffle. To replace it, reverse the operation. It is very simple, and can be learned at once if these instructions are followed. With a snaffle thus treated a leading-rein is formed which will hold the most fractious horse, as, by the rein passing under the jaw, the latter is gagged if the horse tries to get away.

The following maxims should be remembered— viz. :

Never lead a horse on a *bit*.

Never tie up a horse on a snaffle if you have a bit on, as any sudden jerk from a gatepost, railing, or whatever the rein may be attached to might cause a snaffle to cut a horse's tongue badly, as the post or railing is not like the hand in leading, but dead and unyielding.

Furthermore, on no account ever permit your horses to be ridden without a saddle, for the following excellent reasons :

1. The groom wears out his clothes sooner.

2. He is apt to wear out himself. The latter does not so much matter (?).

3. He is very likely to tumble off, and your horse run away and get damaged.

4. Such practices are the very common cause of sore backs to horses.

I can say no more ; there is, perhaps, no necessity for me to do so. But grooms are very fond of thus riding, and think it looks smart and indicates fine horsemanship; and it saves a *little* trouble. That is *their* way of looking at it.

Where horses are in the habit of being *led* at exercise, the leading side should be constantly changed; otherwise their mouths are liable to become hard on one side, and thus a 'one-sided' mouth is formed.

The price of a watering bridle of a good pattern is about 10s. 6d.

PART II.

COACHHOUSE AND SADDLE-ROOM.

CHAPTER XII.

Coachhouse.—Heating coachhouse.—Watering floor of coachhouse.—Flooring of coachhouse.—Saddle-room.—Doors of saddle-room.—Stove of saddle-room.—Patent stove.—Light from window of saddle-room.—Panelling walls of saddle-room.—Disposal of saddlery in saddle-room.—Saddle-racks.—Our patent saddle-racks.—Construction of saddle-racks.—Advantage of saddle-racks.—Prices of saddle-racks.—Saddle-room shelves.—Saddle-room cupboards.—Order and cleanliness.—Forage store.—Disposal of forage in store.—Economy of order.—Bedding-sheds.—Economy and construction of bedding-sheds.—Grooms' chambers.—Communicating window from grooms' chambers to stable.—Comfort of servants' rooms.—Cleanliness of servants' rooms.—Inspection of servants' rooms by master.

I HAVE up to the present confined my attention to the stable itself, and things pertaining to it, alone. I have done so for the purpose of keeping the several parts of this work as distinctly separate as possible. Where there is a stable there is generally a coachhouse and other rooms; I think, therefore, it will be as well to turn to the consideration of these at the present time. Of course, when a stable is built, the following are generally constructed,

either with it or near to it. As a rule, they are generally under the same roof—viz. :
Coachhouse,
Saddle-room,
Forage-house (or loft),
Grooms' chambers,
and (at times) a shed for the purpose of drying stable-litter.

The situation of the coachhouse must, of course, be subservient to that of the stable, and the space available for the purpose. Although a good roomy coachhouse is doubtless an advantage, it should not, as is by no means unfrequently the case, unduly occupy space which can ill be spared from the stable; a somewhat small coachhouse and a roomy stable being more desirable than a large coachhouse and a cramped stable. But whatever situation or size may be selected for a coachhouse, it *must* be *dry*. It need not necessarily be kept *warm*, but the very slightest damp must be excluded. If it is desired to heat a coachhouse, hot-water pipes are undoubtedly the best for the purpose; but they should be so arranged that the heat is generally diffused, and not greater on one side than another. Where this mode of heating is impracticable, it is better to have two or three small stoves (oil stoves are the best) rather than one large one. It is quite possible that in an exceptionally hot summer a carriage may become too dry, to the detriment of the woodwork; and the best-seasoned wood will shrink slightly. When such is the case, it is a good plan to occasionally sprinkle a little water on the floor of a coachhouse. An ordinary watering-pot will be found useful for the purpose; but it should have a fine rose, and be sparingly used.

The floor of a coachhouse should be of concrete. No other material is equal to it. A wooden floor is always a dusty floor; bricks absorb damp; asphalt soon wears out, and either cracks or becomes sticky.

The doors should be double, and should be perfectly balanced, and made to swing back on to a self-catch, so as to avoid any slamming-to on a carriage in high wind, etc. It is as well that there should not be any direct communication between the coachhouse and the stable, as the ammonia, etc., from the stable is not calculated to do other than harm.

The saddle-room should be situated as conveniently to the stable itself as is practicable, and there *should* be communication between the two, so as to obviate the necessity for having to carry articles of saddlery or harness from the one to the other, exposed to rain, etc. Where want of space will not allow a passage to intervene between the stable and saddle-room, if the door of the one leads direct into the other, there should be a double door made to fit closely (one covered with baize will answer the purpose), as it is impossible to preserve leather or steel work if exposed to the fumes which must, in a greater or less degree, exude from a stable. A saddle-room should be warm and dry, but never too hot. As a rule, the saddle-room fire is the warmest in the establishment, and is far too good, and the room is far too hot for the preservation of the leather. A stove is better adapted for saddle-room use than an open fire. It diffuses the heat more generally; it is safer, equally handy (if not even more so) to cook such mashes, etc., as may be required, and does not, perhaps, offer quite the same attractions for grooms to loaf and waste their time round it, as they are very apt to do at an open fire. Moreover, it takes up less *wall* room, and certainly *twice* the number of articles can be aired round a stove as in front of a fire.

There is an excellent pattern of a stove lately invented which is, I think, far better than any other which I have as yet seen; but it can only be used for warming purposes, and requires gas to heat it, though I dare say they may also be constructed to burn oil. This stove consists of a number of coils of iron piping, arranged very much in the form of a firework cracker. These coils contain water, which is heated by a gas light below. It takes up a very small space, and gives out a great deal of warmth in a very short time after being lighted. This stove would serve very well to air clothing, etc., by, but has no arrangement whereby any cooking could be performed. There are, however, so many different kinds of stoves which are suitable for saddle-room purposes, which are very excellent in their several ways, that the reader can select for himself; but it is well to remember that the fumes from some stoves discolour brasswork very rapidly, and the use of such, for the sake of the groom, should be avoided. Brasswork is very easily cleaned, but very soon discolours. Plated harness is less liable, perhaps, to soil quickly than brass, but I do not think it ever looks as smart as brass. This is, however, a matter of choice. Plated is, moreover, slightly more expensive than brass.

The best light for a saddle-room is perhaps that obtained from a skylight, but such lights are constantly leaking and getting out of order.

Saddle-rooms should be panelled, or lined with match-boarding, from ceiling to floor. Here, as in the coachhouse, a concrete floor is the best, as rats and mice cannot work through it.

All bridles, etc., should be kept together and hung up on racks, each one separately, and should be protected from dust by means of curtains to draw in front of them. All articles of harness should be similarly kept.

Spare bits and stirrup-irons should be kept in a case with glass doors, and lined with cloth, baize, or some such material. Where this is not practicable, it is a good plan to keep them in a box filled with slacked lime, by which means they will remain bright and free from rust for a number of years —indeed, will actually *improve* in condition. Saddle-racks are usually fixed to the walls of a saddle-room, and are made of wood or iron; in either case they should be painted. I do not altogether approve of them. By their use saddles are apt to be put too much out of the way—are not visible enough; collect dust very readily; are too near the wall; mice (if there are any) can get at them; they run the risk of being neglected if not in constant use, and so moths get into them; and they are not easily got at if required. Moreover, these racks take up a good deal of room, and very much obscure the light.

Being somewhat cramped for saddle-room, and finding that my saddles were suffering from some or all of the above-mentioned evils, I set myself to work to invent an arrangement which would come up to my idea of what was required, and I succeeded in designing a saddle-rack which I consider has done so. This design I handed over to Messrs. Musgrave, of Belfast, Bond Street, etc., the well-known manufacturers of stable fittings, and they have recently patented it, and carried it out most admirably, and I trust it may meet with success. Its description is as follows, viz.: The saddle-rack itself consists of an open framework of wood, and this is made sufficiently long to take some three or four saddles, one behind the other. It is made of two frames, which are hinged together on their upper sides. Crossbars are screwed on, by means of brass pins, to the ends of the frame, and at each end of these bars there is a brass ring. There are folding legs at each end of the rack, which are made to fold up or open, as may be desired. The whole is strung up to the ceiling of the saddle-room, and moves up and down at will by means of pulleys and cords, which are furnished with hooks to attach to the rings on the crossbars. Thus, when lowered to the ground, it stands firmly on four legs, and can then be used, either as a saddle-stand or a harness-cleaning horse ; and when slung up to the ceiling it becomes also a strong, serviceable saddle-rack. I claim for it the following advantages, viz.: being near the ceiling, it is in the dryest part of the room; when lowered to the ground saddles can be rapidly cleaned and *dried* at the same time, and if desired to expedite the latter, a pan of hot ashes placed on the floor below will quickly dry a wet saddle; moths are easily seen, and can thereby be better prevented; mice *cannot* get at them; the condition of each saddle is seen at once when standing underneath them, and if closer inspection is required, it is a simple matter to draw the rack down; they are out of the way, do not obscure the light, and inasmuch as every saddle is at once visible, there is less likelihood of their being neglected or knocked about. I consider them excellent for either large or small establishments. In the former several racks may be used and hung in rows from the ceiling; in the latter they give more room, as they do not take up any permanent ground space.

Each end of the rack is provided with a hook from which to hang reins, etc., for the purpose of cleaning. For officers in the army, who never have any room or place to keep saddles in other than the stable or an overcrowded officers' kitchen (which latter is generally shared by two or three servants), they would prove invaluable, as only those who have experienced what barrack life is can form any idea of the way saddlery gets knocked about under the existing arrangements; and inasmuch as cavalry officers are specially particular as to their general 'turn out,' both in the hunting-field as well as on parade, the keeping things up to mark, when there is so little room for cleaning, etc., becomes a difficult matter, and a source of endless trouble and expense.

The prices of these racks is from 60s. to 75s. for a *three* saddle rack, according to material. I can hardly say how great a convenience I have found the one I have used in my own saddle-room for some time, although it is but a rough affair, having been made by myself as an experiment.

A few shelves, movable if possible, and one or two cupboards, also made so as to be readily taken out for cleaning, or, at all events, with the shelves constructed so as to slide in and out, are requisite. Perhaps an old wardrobe with shelves is as good as anything, and inasmuch as it can so easily be moved, so as to allow of the room being readily and thoroughly cleaned, and stands *off* the floor, it is the *best* arrangement. It is necessary to have some such convenience for the stowing away of small articles, but anything in actual daily use, such as spare bandages, etc., should be kept on the open shelves, and never put away out of sight, as by this means they are preserved in better condition.

Everything which in any way can possibly tend to encourage dust or dirt should be kept down with a strong hand, and whenever an article becomes unserviceable, it should at *once* be repaired, where such is possible, or made away with.

It is obvious that where horses are kept there must be some place wherein to store the food and the straw, etc., required for their use. Very often the room which is provided for this purpose is not only very small, but also unsuitable. A good loft is as good as anything, inasmuch as such are generally dry, and it is of the first importance that the forage-store should be perfectly dry. For *present* use, corn-bins are sufficient for the oats, bran, etc., but as it is as well to buy oats, hay, and straw in *not* too small quantities, it being cheaper considerably to buy them in bulk, a good store is a necessity, and one in which the forage cannot deteriorate in quality from damp, etc.; and it should be roomy, so as to allow of the forage being neatly arranged, instead of being thrown in anyhow, and here, too, there is obviously a right and wrong way of doing it. To begin with, the trusses of hay should be neatly stacked in the *centre* of the store, and not packed against the walls, as the air gets access to each truss, and especially if they are packed with a small space between each truss. If placed near the wall, they may, and probably will, suffer from damp, and will lose condition.

The sacks of oats should be also away from the walls, and kept in regular rows on their *ends*, and should from time to time be turned round, so that it may be ascertained if they are suffering from the ravages of mice or rats, or possible damp. The straw should also be placed ends up in the bundles, and any other forage should be similarly cared for and disposed of.

It takes very little more time to do this than it does to pile the forage in helter-skelter; indeed, it *saves* time in the long-run, and certainly saves money. Order ever was and ever will be economy in everything. A well-ordered establishment is always an economically managed one. There may be possible extravagance, but there can be but little waste; and if this obtains inside the *house*, it does so in no less degree inside the stable, and everything goes on smoothly and mechanically. But it is absolutely necessary for the maintenance of good order that every detail should be carefully overlooked, and no slackness allowed *anywhere*; and a daily visit, if only of five minutes' duration, by the master, to his stable, etc., will go very far towards ensuring everything being as it should be, especially if aided by a quick eye and the knowledge of what is right and what is wrong. If it can possibly be managed, a shed (or some covered place) where soiled litter can be dried, will be found *very* useful, and as the cost of such an erection is not great, it will be, in the long-run, found true economy, inasmuch as it will save a great deal of waste in straw. So much litter is thrown away because it cannot be dried properly, especially in wet weather, and if there is no other place to dry it in, it *must* be either so disposed of, or else dried as best it can be in the stable; and there is *every* reason why the latter place is unsuitable for such an operation, since the effluvium arising from it is by no means desirable.

Straw is in some parts of the country a rather expensive item, and it is worth while to study economy in its use. A very simple structure will suffice for the purpose—a few upright posts and a roof of corrugated iron being all that is required. If a concrete or asphalte flooring can be added, it will be an advantage. If the expense of even such a shed as the above is objected to, a very fair substitute can be made by means of a roofing of hurdles wattled in with straw, or covered over with tarpaulin, or, indeed, any place will do where the air can get to the bedding and the rain cannot.

The proper place for the chambers of stable servants would appear to be near to the horses under their charge. If the saddle-room adjoins the stable, it might be with advantage over the latter, but that is and *must* be dictated by circumstances. I have seen it advocated that there should always be a window into the stable from the groom's chamber, and such, no doubt, is an excellent plan, as it so very frequently happens that something goes wrong in the stable at night, and any noise or disturbance would be readily noticed, and a word to a fretful or fidgety horse will often have the effect of quieting it. Moreover, if there is anything *really* wrong, it can be at once ascertained, and although a lazy groom would think twice before turning out of his bed at night and going down into the stable, he would hardly hesitate to take the trouble to look through a window or shutter which is close at hand. I would suggest that while the furniture for servants' rooms should be as simple as possible, due regard should be paid to their necessary comfort, as when a man has done a good day's work he is entitled to a good night's rest. But the greatest cleanliness and tidiness should be insisted upon, and I would urge that the master himself should make a point of personally inspecting the rooms occupied by his servants, and not infrequently, and at unexpected times, and not consider it beneath his dignity to condescend to go into them. Such inspections are due to the servants themselves, and in his own interest likewise, and I do not think that any sensible person would, on reflection, think otherwise than I do on this subject.

CHAPTER XIII.

Requirements of a good saddle.—Parts of a saddle.—Saddle-trees.—Saddle-seats.—Saddle-fittings.—Saddle-flaps.—Stuffing of saddles.—Panels.—Sweat-flaps.—Good and bad trees.—Cut of saddles.—Straight seats.—Argument in favour of straight seats.—Length of rein obtained by use of straight seats.—Why horses pull less when ridden by ladies.—Knee-rolls *v.* plain flaps.—*Field* correspondence as to knee-rolls and plain flaps.—Use of the leg in riding.—Cavalry riding.—Advantage of knee-rolls.—Major Whyte-Melville on plain flaps.—Girths.—Stirrup-irons.—Saddle-bar stops.—Fitting of stirrup-leathers.—Good saddles.—Best saddles.—Materials used for lining saddles.—Messrs. Whippy's new system of lining saddles.—Saddle-heads.—Numnahs.—Chambering saddles.—Side-saddles and sore backs.—Back-stays.—Cause and prevention of sore backs in ladies' horses.—Proper position for a lady on side-saddle.—Improper seat.—Safety stirrups for ladies.

BEFORE going into detail as regards saddles, it will be, perhaps, as well for us to consider what a saddle really is. As its name implies, it is a seat. It is, in fact, a seat which is placed on the back of a horse for a person to sit upon. It should therefore be (and we will take the feelings of the dumb animal firstly) comfortable to the horse, and also comfortable to the rider. Now, it cannot be comfortable to the horse if it does not fit him; similarly, it must also fit the rider. The saddle, therefore, must be of such a shape that it combines both of these desiderata.

If the shape of a horse's back and the shape of a man be compared, it will be observed that the one is by no means ill-adapted to the other; that a horse is evidently made for the purpose of carrying a man, and a man is made for riding a horse. With these natural advantages to work on, it should therefore not be a difficult matter to interpose a seat between man and horse, which should in its shape follow the lines of the horse's back, and allow the man riding thereon to sit in a perfectly comfortable and unconstrained manner. Strange to say, however, it is by no means an easy matter to procure a saddle which fulfils both of these requirements, the result being that far too frequently the man, the horse, or both suffer.

The nearer a man can sit to his horse the better he can ride, and the better the horse can carry him.

When a saddle does not sit close and fit well, the weight must be necessarily raised, and the higher it is raised the less steady it must be when a horse is in motion; in plain English, the weight—the man—rocks to and fro on the horse's back, very much to his own discomfort and possible damage to his horse. The friction thus set up wears out the horse's back, and establishes a sore, and this effect is in a measure shared by the man. A really good horseman will, it is true, manage to ride on almost any saddle somehow. But the steadiest seat and the greatest care will not prevent a saddle galling a horse's back if the saddle does not fit it properly. It becomes therefore a matter of the greatest importance that a saddle should fit both horse and man as exactly as possible. A sore man is easily cured, but a sore back takes a long time in healing and recovering its proper condition; indeed, there are few things more troublesome to cure, and when a horse's back has once been 'wrung,' it is generally tender in future, and more liable to suffer again in like manner.

Let us therefore examine a saddle, and dissect it, as it were, so as the better to understand its several parts; and they are these, viz. :

The tree, as it is called.

The seat.

The flaps, panels, etc.

We will take them in the order in which I have named them.

The tree of an ordinary saddle should be light and strong. It is made of wood, and may be, for explanation, divided into four separate parts, viz.: the side-boards, the pommel, or head, and the cantle. The two first-named are connected by the two last. The whole, when fitted together and laid on the back of a horse, should fit and follow the lines and curves of the back perfectly and closely, and yet in such a manner that the edges of the side-boards, or any portion of the tree, cannot bear unduly on the back. A well-shaped saddle-tree will fit nearly any ordinary horse, and will remain in its proper place so perfectly that it would be quite possible to ride on it without girths. The tree, as I have said, is made of wood. Now, if it were all carved out of one piece of wood, it is obvious that, in order that its shape may follow that of the horse's back, the grain of the wood would in several places be across, and not run true, and that where this cross-grain existed manifest weakness must result. It is therefore made in several pieces, which are so joined and dovetailed into each other that, whatever the curve required may be, the grain runs true throughout. This system therefore requires to be very carefully and scientifically carried out. The work is also further strengthened by pieces of metal at both head and cantle, which are termed the front and back arches, and these, in a *good* tree, are closely riveted (the rivets being placed about an inch apart) to the wood. The whole of the wooden portion of the tree is covered with a coating of canvas and glue. I should also add that the bars, as they are called, for the stirrups to be fastened on to, and which are also of metal, are *also* riveted on to the side-boards of the tree. So far, the tree is complete, and it will be readily seen that there is a very great deal of skilled labour necessary to make a good tree, and the material *must* also be the best of its kind, inasmuch as it is absolutely necessary to combine strength with lightness. It is therefore impossible to obtain the best tree in a cheap saddle, and either one or other of the above essentials *must* be wanting.

To ride on a naked tree is, of course, impossible. It must therefore be covered both on its upper and lower side. On the former for the rider's sake, on the latter for that of the horse. It is customary to cover the tree with strong webbing. Over this, again, is placed the leather seat, which completely covers the upper part of the tree from end to end, and is cut out to fit it. This seat is usually made of hogskin, and in order to make it less hard and more comfortable, is lightly padded or stuffed. The rest of the seat is made of either hogskin or ordinary leather, and has short flaps, or skirts, as they are called, which serve to protect and cover the stirrup-bars, which would otherwise be exposed. Behind the stirrup-bars the girthing-straps are *also* riveted on to the side-boards.

Over the girthing-straps and *under* the bar-flaps the saddle-flaps are fastened. There are two large leather or hogskin flaps, which are necessary to protect the legs of the rider from rubbing against the sides of the horse, and the latter from being rubbed and galled by the former.

So much for the *outside* of the saddle.

The inside of the tree (that which is next to the horse's back) is furnished with a covering of serge (which is the material most frequently used), or serge covered with linen, and this is stuffed with horsehair in such a manner as to form a cushion between the hard surface of the tree and the back of the horse, and arranged so as to allow the space along the inside and upper portion of the tree to be clear, as also to avoid any pressure of any part of the tree being possible. *More* or *less* than *just exactly* thus much is bad, and this stuffing of hair should *exactly* correspond with the shape of the tree.

Underneath the saddle-flaps are what are called the panels, which are in reality no more than false flaps of soft leather, which are also slightly stuffed with horsehair, and interposed between the flaps proper and the horse, and serve to absorb sweat, and also for the further comfort of both man and horse. The girthing-straps protrude *over* the panels, between them and the flaps. A still further small flap, known as a sweat-flap, is also fixed between the girthing-straps and the panels.

Now, if a tree fits a horse as it should do, it is a comparatively easy matter to stuff a saddle so that it fits the horse exactly. Of course it must be borne in mind that saddle-trees are made somewhat larger than the actual bare measurements of the horse, so as to allow of this intervening stuffing. A good saddler will easily stuff a saddle with a *good* tree to fit as it should, but the best man in the world *cannot* make a *bad* tree fit well. He may succeed in so arranging the stuffing that the saddle will not gall a horse, but such a saddle will *never* ride well, and *must* necessarily be uncomfortable to the rider; neither can he sit down closely and well 'into' his horse, as he should do, and thereby his power over his horse is lessened, as must of necessity also be his pleasure and comfort. Material and shape are of the first importance; the latter, perhaps, of greater importance than the former, inasmuch as if the tree is good a cheaper description of leather for the seat and flaps *may* be used, and such will last fairly well; but that is the only saving of expense which can be entertained in the construction of a saddle without sacrifice of efficiency.

Now, the *shape* of saddles, what may be termed their 'cut,' may and does vary very considerably. To my way of thinking, provided that it is large enough, there should be as little as possible on a horse, whether in the way of saddle or bridle, etc. If a horse is of a good shape, the less he is covered up with leather the better. Some people prefer to have their saddles cut deep, so as to allow them to sit down in a hollow, as it were. I *cannot* say I like a deep-cut saddle. Where a horse has an unusually hollow back, the tree must of course be made on purpose to fit it; but for horses whose backs are of an ordinary shape, I cannot think that a deep-cut seat can possibly fit as well as one which follows the line of the back more closely. Doubtless a very fat man may require a deeper-cut saddle than an ordinary individual, and I do not for a moment wish it to be inferred that there is but one pattern of saddle, for the contrary is very much the case; and I consider that a man should be measured for his saddle, and that such is quite as necessary as that he should be measured for his breeches and boots. But I *do* think that a saddle-seat should be as straight from pommel to cantle as the shape of the rider will admit of its being, inasmuch as his seat will be better, and thereby his control over his horse greater, and being further back on his horse will give him a greater length of rein, which latter will enable him to handle his horse to greater advantage and with more delicacy.

I *did* intend to refer to this particular point later on, but the present seems to me to be so very suitable that I will here take the opportunity of ventilating what may be but my own theory after all, but which is nevertheless one I believe in myself, and one which I think the reader will agree with me that I have good reasons for advancing. I say that a man can handle a horse better, by reason of having more control over him, and with greater delicacy, at the end of a *long* rein, than with a *short* one. My reasons for making this assertion are as follow : A horse, we will suppose, is a hard puller in single or double harness. Now, put that horse in the lead of a coach, and he will scarcely pull *at all*, probably *not at all*. Put him into the 'wheel,' and he is as bad as ever. And why ? Because, I maintain, he is driven with a longer rein. Now, if this is the case in a coach, why should it not, as I am convinced it does, obtain equally in a saddle ? Everybody knows that it is admitted to be generally the fact that a horse which is a puller in saddle will pull less if ridden by a lady than by a man. The reason *always* given is that a lady's hands are so much more delicate and lighter than those of a man. I grant that this often is and may be so. A woman does not perhaps pull at a horse as much as a man, and consequently the horse, feeling that he gets no fun out of it, gives up the game, and *ceases* to pull at her.

But I do not myself consider that this *fully* explains the reason. There *are* men whose hands are as delicate as any woman's, and who are less physically strong than many a woman, and who are as delicate in their handling as any woman could be. Yet with all this, horses will pull at them and overpower them in a way which they would not do with a lady, and there are many women who can so manage horses, and whose hands can be and are brutally severe on a horse's mouth. I have thought over this subject often and deeply, and I have formed the conclusion that the reason is to be found very much in the fact that a woman's seat on her side-saddle is considerably *further back* than a man's is, and that, having a greater length of rein thereby, she has very considerably increased power. It is, perhaps, the combination of *this* and delicacy of touch, and physical weakness maybe; but what I adduce as an *additional* reason has, I am sure, very much to do with the fact. Therefore I maintain that for this, as well as for the other reasons which I have mentioned, a saddle should be cut as straight as possible. A man can sit *back*, too, so much more easily in a straight seat than in a hollow one, and this is perhaps one of the most difficult positions in the art of horsemanship to acquire. Moreover, by so doing he is better enabled to use the proper muscles of his legs —viz., *those on the sides of his calves*.

And while on the subject of saddles, it will be well to compare the advantages and the disadvantages of what are termed 'knee-rolls' and 'plain flaps.'

Until a few years ago the majority of saddles were made with a padding of leather on the front portion of the flaps to support the knee of the rider. These knee-rolls were either made by the leather of the flaps being continued over the padding in one piece, as it were, or else were sewn on separately—'laid on,' as it is termed. But whichever system was adopted, their *use* remained the same; and there is not a shadow of a doubt but that they are of the very greatest use to a horseman, inasmuch as they give an increase of purchase.

Latterly, however, the fashion has been to discard them altogether, and to substitute what I have said are termed plain flaps—that is to say, flaps without any such stuffing whatever.

I somewhat shrink from entering upon this subject at all, for a few years ago, a letter appearing in the *Field*, which was written by a man who had then but recently returned home from abroad, and who was anxious to be in the fashion and to know which of the two to adopt—viz., knee-rolls or plain flaps—I was weak enough to reply to his queries as fully and honestly as I could. My letter produced such a storm of correspondence, and my reasons (which I here give) were so twisted and turned about, and my meaning, which I thought and hoped I had made so clear and simple, so distorted, that I was very sorry I had taken the trouble to put pen to paper. Eventually it evoked a leading article on the subject. I did not make reply to any of the letters, or I should probably have caused still further misunderstanding; but all the same, my reasons were as simple and matter-of-fact as I will endeavour to make them in the present instance, hoping that the reader will be more lenient to me in his judgment, if he disagrees with me, than my unknown correspondents were.

As I stated above, the proper leg-muscles for a

man to use in riding are those which are situated on the *inside* of the calf of the leg, and not those at the *back* of the calf. Now, these muscles are, in the majority of people, latent; but I do not say with *everyone*. If the support given by the use of a knee-roll is taken away, it is evident that a greater strain must be laid on the muscles of the leg; but anyhow, in all cases, the side-muscles should be used—in other words, the *leg* and *foot* of the rider should be *flat* to his horse's side, and it should be kept well *back* in its place, and never allowed to swing forward. If such is the case, a horse is very likely to get spurred on the shoulder when jumping. If *these* side-muscles are braced, the muscles *above* the knee, the *thigh*-muscles, *must* be braced *also*, though it is not inversely so, as the thigh-muscles may be braced and yet those in the lower part of the leg may be comparatively idle; but in order to secure a good, firm, and elegant seat (and the latter will usually follow the former), the grip of the saddle should be maintained by the *whole* of the leg, thereby distributing the pressure required, and minimizing the fatigue of any particular set of muscles. Now, if the support given by the knee-roll be taken away, there must be a tendency (in most people) for the leg to go forward; and in order to prevent this, a greater strain is thrown on the leg-muscles to retain it in its proper position. After a time, and with constant practice, this necessary pressure becomes instinctive, and the absence of the knee-roll is not felt. Where boys have been taught so to ride, they can ride nearly as well without knee-rolls as with. Cavalry men are trained to ride with the *flat* of their legs, as it is with these that their horses are managed, and *not* with their heels or spurs. A cavalry soldier has to carry his sword in one hand and manage his horse with the other *and his legs*; and the latter have to do the greater share of the work; and *with* them he turns, or 'passes,' his horse, forces him into a trot or gallop, and generally supports him—that is to say, his bridle-hand, though aiding his legs in combination with them, is comparatively speaking of *secondary* importance.

Such men, therefore, have the muscles I have referred to brought out, and by constant use matured, and so can ride just as well without knee-rolls as with them, as far as their riding-powers are required: but take, for example, a man who, having been used to ride with knee-rolls all his life, and who, wishing to be in the fashion, is desirous of taking to plain flaps. He purchases a saddle with plain flaps, and, finding that he misses the support of the knee-rolls to which he has been accustomed, seeks to obtain as strong a grip in his new saddle as he had in his old one, and so, in order to secure it, he turns the *back* of his calf into the saddle, so as to obtain from the fulness of his calf the muscles which should be sufficient, if they were *present*, on the side of his leg. The *back* of his calf being into his saddle, his toes must turn out, and very ugly and ungainly his seat becomes. As a consequence to this, though why I cannot explain, up go his hands and out go his elbows. Now, this is no exaggeration. I only ask the reader to take notice for himself, and if he does so he will see the truth of what I say.

Personally, I always use plain flaps. I like the look of them; they show off a horse's shoulder better. They last longer, and look more sportsman-like; and I *can* ride in them, having had so many years of cavalry service; but if asked if I consider that my seat is as *perfectly* strong in them as in a 'knee-rolled' saddle, I at once reply, 'Certainly not.' When does one ever see a man ride a steeplechase in a small saddle *without* knee-rolls, and *why?* The question, I think, answers itself sufficiently.

That best of good sportsmen and horsemen, the late Major Whyte-Melville, urges in favour of plain-flapped saddles that they are easier to get back into if a man should be thrown at all forward from his saddle, and so get his legs in front of it. I respect and admire *all* he has ever said and written; but I would ask this question, or, rather, I should say, make this remark, viz. : A man has no right to *get* into such a position. Probably he would not have got there if he had a knee-roll on his saddle to keep him back.

As an accompaniment to saddles are the girths; and there are several descriptions of these. The girths in most general use are double; that is, simply two girths made of broad webbing, and furnished with double buckles at each end, which are sewn on with strong leather 'tabs.' These webbing girths are made in various colours—white, blue, or fawn being those commonly used. If there *is* a choice of any particular colour, I should feel inclined to give the preference to the white, as they are so easily cleaned and pipeclayed, and always look clean and smart, and the blue fades very soon, and consequently has a shabby appearance. The fawn shows stains which cannot very easily be got out, and so looks dirty.

Of the various patterns of girths, that called the Fitzwilliam is by far the best, though rather more expensive than the others. It consists of one extra-broad girth of webbing, with *two* double buckles at each end; and over this, again, there is another narrower girth with only one buckle at either end. There are standing runners (leather loops) sewn on to the broader girth, to keep the narrower one in its place. The advantages derived from the use of these girths are that they are stronger, and that there can be no possible chance of nipping or pinching a horse with them, as there is with the ordinary double girths. There are, in addition to the above-named, girths which are made of raw hide, plaited, and of leather, plaited in the same way; but I have not found them altogether satisfactory. It is true that they are *very* strong, almost unbreakable, and that a horse cannot get pinched or girth-galled with them, and that, the plaits being separate and joined together at wide intervals by pieces of leather, through the loops of which they are made to run, they are very cool; but they are very troublesome at first, as they stretch so much; and until they have been by long use stretched to their *utmost*, they require constant alteration or shortening; and as this has to be done by a saddler, it becomes very inconvenient. When once they are fully stretched (and nothing but use will thoroughly effect this), I have nothing but praise to say in their favour. The better description of the two, the raw hide, continue to stretch much longer than the leather ones. A girth should be just tight enough to allow a finger's breadth between it and the horse.

Stirrup-irons are of great variety. I pin my faith to those which are *plain*; but they should have what are called 'Prussian sides,' viz., should be made wide where the arch joins the foot-bar, so as to prevent the foot being bruised by reason of the round iron pressing against the outside of it, and a *round* arch can make itself very uncomfortable at the end of a long day's hunting, when the foot has necessarily been 'home' in the stirrup for many hours. The term 'home' implies that the *whole* foot is thrust into the stirrup as far as it will go, and that the bar of the stirrup is under the hollow of the foot therefore, and not under the ball of it. Such irons as I have described look smarter, and are workmanlike also.

There are *no end* of other stirrup-irons which have been from time to time invented as safety stirrups. They are all doubtless excellent in their way, and bear out the good qualities they are declared to possess; but I do not care for them, and, as I have said, I prefer the *plain* ones, but these latter *must fit* the foot of the rider, and be neither too large nor too small in *any* measurement, whether in height of arch or width of bar. If they are too large in either of these, it is by no means impossible or improbable that the foot of the rider may, should his horse fall with him, slip through the stirrup, and so he may get dragged and sustain serious injury. On the other hand, a similar result may occur if it is too small, as his foot may get wedged in, and he may not be able to extricate it. As stirrup-irons are made in various sizes, it becomes an easy matter to secure those which fit properly.

The springs of the stirrup-bars, etc., which are fixed on the saddle, should never be fastened, but always be kept *down*. The reader will easily see what I refer to if he will take the trouble to look at any saddle. On lifting up the bar-flaps he will see that at the end of them there is a spring-catch, which opens or closes the bar, in order to allow the stirrup-leathers to be passed in on to the bars. It is this spring-catch which should be kept open. The reason for this is obvious, and there is but little chance of being dragged, if thrown, if this advice is followed. If the 'stops,' as they are called, are up, the chances are much in favour of a very nice and complete accident, with a full amount of damage, being secured. These stops are really useless, as the stirrup-leather will remain in its place quite as well as is required without them, and I would advise the reader never to get into a saddle without first looking under the bar-flap on *each* side, and making sure that the stops are *down*.

It is a great nuisance to most people to have to alter the length of the stirrups *after* mounting, and especially if a horse is at all fractious, and, if I may be pardoned for saying so, I always think a man looks such a helpless fool when he is slewed round in his saddle while the groom is altering the stirrup-irons or girths for him, the horse, perhaps, meanwhile dodging about all over the place. In order to prevent this, the following rough guide serves to show pretty accurately the proper length of stirrup for ordinary people, according to their height, length of leg, etc. If a man has long legs, he generally has long arms, and arms and legs are much of the same character in each individual. Now, if it is desired to gauge the length of stirrup required, adopt the following plan : Stand facing your saddle, take up the stirrup-iron with one hand, and, drawing it out to the full length of the leather, measure it with the other arm ; the fingers of the hand of the measuring arm should be extended till they touch the stirrup-bar. The foot-bar of the stirrup-iron should touch the side of the body under the armpit. If too long, shorten, if too short, lengthen, the stirrup-leathers till they are the exact measurement. They will, on mounting, be found to be the required length. The price of a good London saddle is about six guineas, or perhaps slightly less.

It is better to purchase a second-hand saddle by a really good maker, if it is in good condition and *fits*, than to obtain a new one for possibly the same price from an inferior maker.

The best London saddlers are these: Messrs. Whippy, Merry, Souter, and Wilkinson and Kidd. I do not think that there is any choice between any of these: all are as good as they can possibly be. There are doubtless numerous others also, but these hold the 'pride of place' in the trade, and the reader may be perfectly certain of obtaining from either of them the very best cut, workmanship, and material in the whole of the civilized world. They will, moreover, fit him and his horse too. *If they cannot, no one can.*

I have observed that white serge is the material most generally used for the lining of saddles, panels, etc., and such is the case. I do not, however, wish to infer that I consider it the best material which can be used for the purpose, inasmuch as they are very frequently covered with linen, and very advantageously so too, especially where horses are very sensitive in their backs; and I therefore consider the latter better in every case, as if it saves a *tender* back it *must* also be more comfortable, generally speaking. It is cool and smooth, wears quite as well as serge, and, what is more, is not so attractive to moths, and I should advocate its use.

Within the last few years Messrs. Whippy, of London, have brought out a new method of lining saddles. I have never used it myself, but I have seen it. I hear nothing but the highest praise respecting it. It is this: All serge or linen lining is completely done away with; the tree is covered with thick felt, and over this there is a covering of plain, smooth leather; the seat is also lined with leather in a similar manner. Beyond this there is apparently nothing, and apparently nothing further is required. As may be supposed, the rider is able by its use to sit very close to his horse, and that alone is a very great desideratum. Saddles so lined are comparatively indestructible, and are, of course, very much lighter, while the lightness obtained is not in any way at the expense of strength or durability. I am given to understand that Messrs. Whippy have not in any way patented or protected this improvement, and I have recently seen one which has been made by Mr. Orpwood, of Oxford, and which is an improvement on the ordinary way of fixing such lining. I tried a saddle lined with leather, as I have described, on a saddler's horse, and I must say that, although such a method of trying a saddle is by no means as satisfactory as the actual animal itself, I was fully convinced of the very great additional grip which must be obtained by using saddles so treated, as also of their apparent comfort to the rider.

In order to keep the leather lining soft and supple, nothing further than a little soap is required, and I should say that they must be charming to ride on, and should be equally comfortable for even the most tender-backed horse, and I am assured that such is the case.

I had almost forgotten to make mention regarding the head of a saddle—the 'pommel,' as it is generally called—but I can do so here as well as elsewhere. In some provincial, but nowadays in no well-made London saddles, the head of the saddle is cut back towards the seat, and is what is termed 'cow-mouthed.' Now, this is wrong altogether, and positively dangerous, and no hunting-saddle should ever be so made, and I am inclined to believe that a good London saddler would refuse to sell a saddle of such a shape. I will ask the reader to follow me in supposing that he has the misfortune to be thrown slightly forward in his saddle against the head of a saddle with a 'cow-mouth.' Let him but look at such a saddle; he will be able to judge for himself what amount of injury he could very easily sustain. On the other hand, let him examine one with a straight head, and he will see that the gullet-iron of the saddle being further away from him, the danger is lessened, and that the *shape* of the latter is also of a less harmful character than the former. *Either* would be bad enough, but the one would be infinitely worse than the other.

It is sometimes the custom to use what is called a 'numnah,' which is a kind of saddle-cloth, for the purpose of protecting a horse's back when such is inclined to be tender; but if a saddle fits a horse properly and is properly lined, as I have endeavoured to explain it can and should be, such an addition is unnecessary. I will, however, explain that numnahs are made of felt, sheepskin, and leather. Either of these answers the purpose. The latter is, however, the most workmanlike, but it must be kept soft with soap; and, indeed, care and the most perfect cleanliness is necessary with all three descriptions, otherwise they are apt to get hard and lumpy, and to cause the very evil they are intended to avert.

Where a horse's back has been at all galled, and it is inconvenient to throw him out of work, the saddle may be 'chambered'—that is to say, a hollow formed in that part of it which would otherwise bear on the sore, by removing some of the stuffing and sewing round the base of the hollow thus created; but this must, of course, be done by a saddler, and carefully done, too. And the saddle must be girthed very exactly, so as to ensure the 'chambering' being over the exact spot, and not shifting; otherwise the sore will be very considerably increased, and the horse thereby have to be laid up for some long time. But, to speak plainly, such a thing as a sore back should be unknown in a properly managed stable.

Ladies' horses are more subject to sore backs than others, and for the following reasons—viz.: A side-saddle is longer in the seat than a man's saddle, and being so it is more apt to swing from side to side and cause a sore. Where such is the case, the sore is generally on the near side of the back; and very often another is also formed at the same time on the off side of the withers. And in order to prevent this swaying to and fro it is necessary to use a back-stay, as it is called, which is a divided strap fastened from the off and outer edge of the tree and the seat of the saddle, and connected with the surcingle. There are various ways of arranging this back-stay; but a back-stay is necessary, especially for hunting purposes. Mr. Souter, of the Haymarket, has invented an arrangement by which the trees of side-saddles are very much strengthened, by means of an iron or steel band which is placed transversely across the tree from the near side of the shoulder to the off-side seat, and which there terminates in a D for the attachment of the back-stay. If my memory serves me aright, I think I have described this accurately, although it is some years since he was kind enough to explain it to me.

If it is necessary for a man's saddle to fit well, it is perhaps, if possible, more so, that a side-saddle should fit, and that the seat should be as straight as it can be. Naturally, the straighter the seat the longer the saddle: hence an additional reason for the use of a back-stay with a side-saddle, and also because, as a woman's seat on a horse is very much an artificial one, she is therefore entirely dependent for her strength of seat on her saddle *alone*, as, apart from her *balance*, the only hold she can obtain is that which is afforded by the pommels. A woman should sit fair and square *on* her saddle, and not on the side of it. How many women are there who do so? Or, rather, how few there *are!* Her shoulders, when mounted, should be perfectly square to the front, and her foot should be perfectly flat to the side of her horse, and at whatever pace she may be riding, this position should be maintained. It was well-nigh impossible in the old deep-cut saddles, in which the head was so high, for this to be the case without the very greatest exertion and consequent fatigue. In a straight-seated saddle, however, the case is different, and there is no reason why a proper seat, such as I have described, should not be acquired. Too often, alas! is it the case that as soon as a horse begins to trot, and the lady rises to it, she does so sideways, and not truly forwards; and her foot goes kicking out in a fashion by no means graceful, although both rider and foot may be everything which is charming. The result of this sideways movement is that the saddle receives a side-twist, and the wretched horse gets the benefit of it, generally in two places at once—viz., the off wither and near side of the back. My reason, therefore, for laying extra stress on the necessity of side-saddles fitting well, and the use of a back-stay with them, is, I conclude, very apparent.

As regards stirrups for side-saddles, I say, By all means use anything which is best calculated to avoid an accident. A woman is so at the mercy of her horse, she is necessarily so encumbered with her habit (no matter how well it may fit, or how ingeniously it may be arranged, there is still a great amount of cloth which can catch on pommels, etc.), and the sight of a lady being 'dragged' is so terrible, that if danger to her can in *any way* be lessened, in mercy's name let it be so by all means !

I love to see good horsewomen, but I am always anxious for their safety, especially in the hunting-field. It has been my lot to pilot more than one brilliant horsewoman to hounds, and amongst them one very dear to me—no other than my wife ; but such hunting-days have ever been the reverse of pleasurable to me, by reason of my intense anxiety, knowing how little causes an accident, and how dire such may prove to a lady rider to hounds.

CHAPTER XIV.

Bridles. — Headstalls. — Buckles. — Browbands. — Reins. — Parts of a bridle.—Double-rein snaffles.—Bits.—Shape of a horse's mouth.—Hard and soft mouths.—Spoiled mouths.—How to fit a bit in a horse's mouth.—Curb.—Throat-lash.—Noseband.—Variety of bits.—The temptation of a saddler's shop.—Fancy bits.—Useful bits.— Useless bits. — Snaffles. — Use of two snaffles. — Gag-snaffles.—Bits and bridoons.—Too severe bits.—The gridiron.— Curb-save.—Lip-straps.— Ward-bits.— Bit-mouthpieces.—Instrument for measuring a horse's mouth.—The 'Pelham' bit.—'Ben Morgan' bit.—'Ben Morgan' bit for driving. — Breast-plates.—Fitting of breast-plates.— Martingales. — Standing-martingales. — Rein-rings. — How to saddle a horse.—Cleaning of saddlery.—Evils of saddle-paste.—Care in cleaning saddle-flaps.—Prices of saddlery.

THE appearance of a horse is very much improved or marred according as his bridle is well or ill cut or put on.

There should not be one scrap of leather on a horse's head more than is absolutely necessary to secure the proper amount of strength. I hardly know which looks the worse, a heavy head-stall with over-broad, clumsy-looking leathers, or one which is too much the other way. As in all things there is a happy medium, so is there in the present instance; and the happy medium is here as elsewhere—after all but common-sense. Both headstall and reins should be invariably sewn on to the bit, for the reasons I have given before when making mention of watering bridles; and all buckles should be of plated metal, and *not* covered with leather. The leather should be of its own natural colour, and not coloured with saffron or any such stuff, as is often the case with cheap saddlery. As a rule, only one rein, the snaffle, is made to buckle in its middle; but I think it an advantage to have a buckle on both snaffle and bit reins. As I have before observed in another part of this book, it is *quite inadmissible* to use any coloured browband; nothing but plain leather, the same as the reins, should ever be worn. All reins, excepting those which are used with a gag-snaffle, should be flat. One not infrequently sees ladies' bridles made with round reins, and at times there is also an addition in the shape of a sort of tassel of leather which hangs under the horse's throat, and perhaps a fringe of leather adorning the horse's nose. Can bad taste extend further? One always looks for the green velvet habit, long white gauntlets, and spangles of the circus-rider also. Of late years, I am glad to say, this sort of adornment has very much gone out of fashion, and women are more sensibly attired, both on and off horseback; and they turn out better, and, I may add, ride better, too, than in former days, and such monstrosities in the way of saddlery as the above are going out of fashion.

A bridle consists of the following parts, viz.: headstall, browband, reins, throat-lash, and (at times) a noseband; but this latter is only used where necessary to keep a horse from 'yawing' his mouth open, and when used is better fitted on its own headstall—what is called a headstall noseband. Where a snaffle only is used the headstall is single; but where an ordinary double bit, bit and bridoon, or curb and snaffle (and it is called by all three names), is worn, then the headstall is double, one portion being for the snaffle, and the other for the bit, and there are, of course, reins attached to both bit and snaffle.

As a rule, snaffles are, and should be, furnished with double reins when used alone, as they are, of course, safer than a single rein could be.

There are nearly as many different kinds of bits as there are days in the year. I think before I enter upon the subject of them (and I only intend to refer to those which are practical, and not fancy bits) it will be as well if I endeavour, in as few words as possible, and as simply as I can, to explain to the reader what a horse's mouth really is like. Possibly he has never taken the trouble to look or inquire. It is furnished with teeth, palate, and a tongue, like that of all other quadrupeds. The teeth are divided in both the upper and lower jaws into two distinct and separate sets, as are our own, only that in the horse there is a space between the two sets—the 'gatherers,' or front teeth, and the 'grinders,' or back teeth. As may be inferred, the duty of the former is to bite off and collect the grass upon which, in its natural state, a horse would feed; that of the latter to grind the food thus collected. The gatherers, or front teeth, are six in number—six in the upper and six in the lower jaw. The grinders are also six in number on each side of each jaw, thus making in all twelve gatherers, or, as we may call them, front teeth, and twenty-four grinders, or back teeth. Between these front and back teeth there is a space of some three inches. In the adult *mare* this space remains blank. In the *horse* there is a tusk, or 'tush,' as it is called, an inch above the corner front tooth, on either side of each jaw. What its use is I cannot say, but we may be sure that it is there for *some* wise purpose. At times, and by no means infrequently, this tusk is found present in the mouth of a mare. Whether the presence of this tooth in the mouth of a mare is a sign of sterility I am not in a position to state, as I have never taken the trouble to ascertain, although it has often occurred to me that such may be the case. With this preamble I may proceed.

In a young horse the mouth is naturally tender —in other words, every horse is born with what is called a good mouth. It rests, therefore, entirely with the breaker as to whether that mouth is spoiled (hardened) or not. It is also true that all horses have not the same temperament; where one is quiet and docile and easily broken, another is equally impatient of control, and fights against the bit which is placed in his mouth; and here the patience and delicacy of touch which a good horse-breaker should possess is called into play. Every abrasion of the tender mouth by the steel of the bit tends to harden a horse's mouth, until, in the hands of a man who is wanting in either touch or temper, it becomes callous, and the horse's mouth is spoiled and he is *taught* to pull. It may therefore be rightly argued that where a horse is a puller his mouth has been spoiled by bad handling, though I have fully proved to my own satisfaction that it is quite possible by a long course of gentleness and patience to do very much towards restoring the tenderness which should exist in a horse's mouth.

Now it will be well to explain how a bit should be placed in the mouth of a horse so as to be least annoying to him, and also give the rider the greatest control over him. The following simple rules, as laid down for the bitting of cavalry horses, will be found sufficient for all practical purposes :

The snaffle should fit the horse's mouth so as to touch the corners of the mouth lightly, but without creasing or gagging them. The bit should be placed so that the mouthpiece should rest on the bars (the gums) one inch above the tusk in a *horse*, and two inches above the corner tooth (the last of the gatherers, or front teeth) in a *mare*.

The curb-chain should be loose enough to admit the *breadth* of at least one finger between it and the jawbone.

The throat-lash should be loose enough to admit the breadth of three fingers between it and the side of the jaw.

The noseband (if one is used) should be placed so as to be the breadth of two fingers below the projection on the cheek-bone of the upper jaw, and loose enough to admit two fingers'-breadth between it and the lower jaw.

'Circumstances alter cases,' but that is the fitting

of a bridle for an ordinary bit for an ordinary horse, and it cannot be improved upon, whether for a snaffle or for a double bit.

And now as to the bits themselves. As I said, their name is legion. Let the reader at once make up his mind to be content with a few simple bits; the fewer he can do with the better, always provided he has enough for his requirements. No woman in a milliner's shop is more tempted to buy what she does not want than is a man in that of a saddler. Therefore do not go and buy everything and anything which may be the latest invention, especially in the way of bits. They will prove but useless lumber, and are not worth the expense, or even the trouble, of keeping in order. Fancy bits are only fit for one purpose, and that is for the saddler to sell. If a horse will not go in a simple bit, the chances are that he will not go any better in a fancy one. For a *little* time he may, until he becomes used to its action; but after a time he generally learns to dodge the new arrangement as well as the old one, and he pulls as hard as ever. Make up your mind to either stick to him and endeavour to cure him by good handling and by fair means, or else to get rid of him.

I intend to put only the following bits on my list, viz. :

The snaffle.
Ordinary bit and bridoon.
'Pelham.'
'Ben Morgan.'

All other bits I set aside as being more or less fancy bits, and not adapted for the use of ordinary people, and also as being either too severe for any but the most finished horsemen to use, or utter rubbish.

Snaffles may be classed as follows, viz. : Plain, twisted, and gag—and whichever of these they may be, the mouthpiece should be large, so as not to cut the corners of a horse's mouth. A plain snaffle is made perfectly plain and smooth in the mouthpiece, which latter is jointed in the middle.

A twisted snaffle has the two pieces forming the mouthpiece twisted. Either of these may be made with single or double rings (the latter is the more powerful and the better pattern), or with check-pieces, which may be made to fit into a standing loop on the check-strap of the headstall, in which case they are generally made *flat*, or to act independently. The former is a good plan, and gives a slightly increased bearing, and keeps the bit from working through the mouth.

A plain snaffle is the very lightest description of bit there is; and a horse which will go well, and what is termed 'wear' himself well, in a snaffle, must be possessed of a perfect mouth; and it is the best and safest bit to use for hunting, especially in a bank country, where it is essential that a horse should not have his mouth interfered with unduly, and be able to extend himself as fully as he finds it necessary. It has been remarked by one of the best horsemen the world has known, that but few horses are well mouthed and mannered enough to be ridden in a snaffle, and but fewer men possessed of hands good enough to use a bit. If that were the case, most people would have to give up riding altogether—but his meaning is of course apparent.

Where one single snaffle is not sufficient for a horse, and he is 'dead' on it, two may (what is termed) advantageously be used. In which case one of them may be twisted, and the other plain, and, of course, in this case there would be but a single rein attached to each. By the use of two snaffles, as thus described, all 'deadness' of the mouth is avoided, for if a horse bears on the one, the other can always be brought into play, and thus a constant change kept going, and without damaging his mouth. It is in fact a good movable mouthful, and I often wonder that such an arrangement is not more frequently made use of.

A gag-snaffle, as its name implies, gags the mouth, and is constructed so as to draw up the corners of the mouth when the reins (which are made round at that portion of its length) are drawn tight, the round part being made to run through two metal eyes, which are fixed on what are best described as cheek-pieces, or shanks. Such a bit is, however, only used in special cases, and in order to keep a horse's head up and prevent his boring, and is never used alone, but in connection with either another plain snaffle or a bit, and is not a thing to be used by just anybody with impunity. I very nearly killed myself when riding a steeplechase through being forced against my will to use a gag-snaffle. I lost the race and, as I say, nearly lost my life. I *ought*, had I been wise, to have refused to ride; moreover, the gag was a bad one of its kind, and did not run smoothly and properly, as it should have done. If properly made and fitted, and used carefully and with discretion, a gag is for ordinary purposes, at times, exceedingly useful, but in bad hands exceedingly dangerous. It is, however, the only bit I know of which will keep a horse's head up if he is a persistent borer, but, like the oft-repeated answer to queries in the

Field regarding the use of biniodide of mercury, 'it must be used sparingly.'

The ordinary bit, snaffle and curb, or bit and bridoon, as it is called, consists of a steel mouthpiece, with what is termed a port in the centre of it; in other words, it rises up in the centre in an arch. This arch or port is made high or low, according as the bit is more or less severe. The higher the port, the more severe its action, and *vice versâ*. The mouthpiece is made with a shank or cheek at either end of it, and the two are welded together. At the upper end of the shanks are round eyes, to which the headstall is sewn on. The lower ends are furnished with loose rings for the reins. Two swinging hooks are attached (one on either side) to the upper eyes, for the purpose of fastening on the curb-chain, which passes round under the jaw. The action of the bit is therefore a double one—viz., that of the port upwards, and that against the curb-chain downwards, the mouthpiece forming a powerful lever against the lower jaw, which is forced upwards by the curb-chain. This double action may be very much increased by the use of longer shanks on the bit, by a tighter curb-chain, and by, as I have already remarked, a higher port.

I cannot recommend the use of anything excessive in the above. The bit becomes too severe, and is dangerous for ordinary use. I am aware that there *are* people who are gifted with such perfect hands that they can ride with anything, and one of our best gentlemen horsemen habitually uses a bit with a port like a gridiron, and such, indeed, it is called, and *he can* use it; but then there are very few men in England who can ride and handle a horse as he can—certainly *none better*—and if I were to mention his name, the fact would be admitted by all who know him, or *of* him. He rides big, well-bred horses, and strongly objects to being pulled at, and so tackles them in this way, and can handle them over the biggest part of Leicestershire in the most masterly style.

An ordinary bit should be large in the mouthpiece. The curb-chain should be large in the links, and what is called a curb-save may be used with advantage. This latter is a piece of leather which has loops sewn on to it, and through which the curb-chain is passed. It is used for the purpose of protecting the horse's jaw, and preventing its being cut by the broad steel links of the chain. In any case where a bit is used, a lip-strap should be added. It is a very simple arrangement, and consists of a round leather strap, which is buckled on to either shank of the bit by means of two small eyes, with which, I had omitted to observe, the shanks of bits are provided for the purpose. This strap passes through a loose ring in the centre of the curb-chain, and serves to prevent a horse throwing his bit up over his nose —a habit which many horses acquire, and which would constantly occur, were it not for this precaution, with a fidgety horse which tosses his head about.

I have said that a snaffle is the safest bit to use for hunting in a bank country, and so it is. There is, however, a bit which is much used in Ireland, and which is there called the 'Ward' bit. It has a *very* low port and very short shanks, the latter almost shorter than the width of the mouthpiece. There are many people who profess to like them. I cannot say that I see any advantage in them, inasmuch as they are useless as bits, and no better than a good snaffle, and they most certainly do not look well. They always make me think that those who use them do so because they may pull at them with impunity, and that they either dislike the use of a snaffle or are afraid to use a proper bit. Anyhow, they do no *harm*, which is *more* than can be said of many bits. The mouthpiece of a bit should be amply wide enough for a horse's mouth, so as to ensure that the corners of the mouth are not pinched in by the shanks, and yet not wide enough to allow of the bit rolling about from side to side.

I believe that in the German cavalry they use a gauge to measure the mouths of the horses, so as to get the exact width. Such a gauge is doubtless a very useful thing to horses, but as we do not find it necessary in our own cavalry, its use may be dispensed with in an ordinary stable, and such very accurate measurement is by no means imperative.

There is a bit called a 'Pelham,' and it is a bit which many people run down, because they assert that it is neither bit nor snaffle—neither the one thing nor the other—and what they say is quite true; and yet its very merit is that it *is* neither the one nor the other, inasmuch as where a snaffle is not quite strong enough for a horse, and a bit is too much, a 'Pelham' is the very thing required. It is, in fact, a bit with the mouthpiece of an ordinary snaffle, instead of the fixed bar of an ordinary bit, the mouthpiece being jointed in the middle like a snaffle, and the shanks made to use with a curb-chain the same as a bit. For thoroughbred horses which pull a little bit too much to be pleasant to ride with a snaffle, it is the very best bit I know, and a very safe one to use also ; and no stable should be without one where more than two or three horses are kept, as there is sure to be one horse at *least* which it would suit.

Ben Morgan, who for many years was huntsman to the Pytchley (and no better ever carried a horn), invented a bit which bears his name, and a very excellent bit it is, especially for horses which pull or carry their heads too high, or for horses whose heads are badly or heavily set on. It is, to all appearances, when on, like an ordinary bit, but the mouthpiece, instead of having a port in it, is perfectly round and smooth, and is made in a slight curve from cheek to cheek, *with the curve lying downwards towards the horse's teeth*—like what is called a half-moon bit, only *reversed*. As the mouthpiece is low in the horse's mouth in the centre only, it therefore bears on the tongue, and, moreover, prevents a horse from getting ' dead ' in hand, as he, trying to reach it, plays on it, and so yields his head to the hand of the rider. It is perfectly smooth and simple in its action, and does not cut or bruise a horse's mouth, inasmuch as it obtains by, as it were, cajolery what cannot be secured by force. It is necessary that, in order to obtain the full advantage of its action, the curb-chain should be as slack as it reasonably can be. I know but one thing against it, which is, that if a horse is inclined to bore it is apt to make him bore rather than prevent his doing so; but in order to obviate this, a brother officer of mine, Captain (now Major) Haynes, contrived a combination of running gag to use with it instead of the ordinary snaffle, and he got Mr. Cooper, the saddler in York (who had, I believe, at one time the monopoly for the sale of the 'Ben Morgan' bits, and, indeed, may still have it, for aught I know to the contrary), to carry it out for him; and it is a most excellent arrangement, inasmuch as the bit acting downwards, and the gag upwards, the horse's head is thereby kept steady. Of course, where a horse does not bore this combination is unnecessary, and the ordinary snaffle can be used. I have used it myself, and can vouch for its good qualities, and was enabled by its use to hunt with the most perfect comfort a horse which I could not hold with any other bit, and whose mouth was as hard as a paving-stone. I can also answer for its good qualities as a driving-bit. I was not aware, for some time after I purchased the one referred to, that such bits were made for use in harness. At the time we had, as wheeler in our regimental coach, a horse which, as a puller, I believe was never beaten. Many a time have I cursed the day he was foaled, for he was surely the most inveterate puller which ever looked through a collar;

but he was such a rare good-looking horse, and such a wonderful worker, that we could not afford to part with him. We bought him as being a notorious puller, and we bought his bit with him too—such a bit as it was, with a port like a fire-shovel, added to which we were obliged to put a roughed curb-chain inside his mouth, and another one, also roughed, under his jaw, and this state of things we endured for a long time.

One St. Leger meeting I chanced to come across an old schoolfellow who, like myself, was also driving his regimental coach, and we fell to talking over coaching matters. I knew his team (which, by the way, were as good a lot of horses as could be got together) were a bit hard-mouthed, and wondered that he, having met with a severe accident to his left arm, could hold them; and then he told me that he always used 'Ben Morgan' bits on the pullers, and advised me to get one for our headstrong wheeler. I followed his advice, and discarded all the former instruments of torture, and from that time forward was able to drive in comfort. I may also add that I have for some years past used it on a pony which I have, and which I bought as being quite impossible to hold; and she was *quite* so, until I ordered a 'Ben Morgan' bit for her. Since then she has given me no trouble, and a child can drive her with the most perfect ease.

Should it ever be the reader's fortune to be troubled with a hard-pulling horse, I can most confidently and strenuously urge him to profit by these experiences.

A breast-plate is necessary in the hunting-field alone, and even there its use is being abandoned, since, as its purpose is to keep a saddle from slipping back, it is not required save in hilly countries, and for horses which are light-ribbed, and whose conformation in this respect favours the working back of the saddle. It is now the fashion to discard them in Leicestershire, inasmuch as it is *de rigueur* to eschew one particle of unnecessary saddlery ; and certainly, if there is no use for them, why retain them ? I must admit, however, that I am conservative, or old-fashioned enough to like them, and there must, in my opinion, be times when they are useful. They always to me seem to be the badge of a hunter.

For the information of the reader, I will endeavour to describe what a breast-plate is. A loose collar formed of a leather strap about an inch wide, which, passing over the withers of the horse, is joined together above the breast-bone, and is there met by a broader strap, which latter passes between

BREAST-PLATE.

the forelegs and is fastened to the girth—or rather, I should say, is fastened by the girth—which is run through a loop at the end of the strap, which loop is formed by the end being doubled back on the strap with a buckle, which is made to run according as it is required to lengthen or shorten the breast-plate. The shoulder-pieces and this main-piece are united by means of a ring, to which they are sewn.

The part which rests on the withers is made wider than the side-pieces, and is about a foot in length. This also is connected with the side-pieces by means of a ring at either end, and thus these two rings lie on either side of the withers. Two small straps, one on each side, are also sewn on to these rings, and are buckled on to D's which are fixed on the saddle for the purpose. By this means the saddle is kept steadily forward on the horse's back, and cannot (unless the breast-plate breaks) slip back.

It is, however, very necessary that a breast-plate should be properly put on. The breast-ring should be two inches above the horse's breast-bone. In this position it will be neither too high nor too low. The side-pieces should be loose enough to allow of the *breadth* of a hand between them and the shoulder of the horse. The main-piece should be loose enough to admit of the same measurement as the side-pieces. Strange to say, there is perhaps no article of saddlery which is more generally badly put on than a breast-plate. It is either too tight or too loose. It either cramps the horse (in which case it is very likely to break), or else it is too loose to be of any use. And very often the main-piece is far too long—*dangerously* so; for, if such is the case, it is by no means a difficult matter for a horse which has fallen over a fence to get his foreleg through in his struggles, and such an occurrence would be scarcely likely to mend matters.

Where horses carry their heads too high, it is necessary to adopt some plan to remedy the evil; and this may be done by the use of a 'martingale,' as it is termed, and which is somewhat similar to a breast-plate, but with the addition of two split straps of leather provided with rings, through which the snaffle-reins are passed, and thus the horse's head is drawn and kept down. If it is necessary to use such a martingale, the breast-plate may be utilized by the use of the split straps alone, which may be made to buckle on to the breast-ring. Such a martingale as I have described is termed a 'running martingale,' inasmuch as the reins run through its rings.

There is a description of martingale which is

fixed and does not run, but I cannot advise its use, and especially for hunting purposes, as it is not safe.

A far better and simpler plan is to use two metal rings which are connected by a piece of leather of about six inches in length and one inch broad. The snaffle-reins run through these rings, and when the reins are drawn tight the rings are drawn up under the horse's jaw. This is a great deal safer, and is far more sightly and workmanlike, and answers equally well. This arrangement is sometimes made of metal entirely, without the leather. I must caution the reader against using it, as I have been constantly informed that a horse's throat may, in the struggles of a fall, get badly cut by the metal bars which connect the rings; and this *cannot* occur with the leather.

And now, before closing this already over-long chapter, I will add a few words as to the fitting on of a saddle. It should be placed fairly and truly in the centre of the horse's back, and so as to allow the width of a hand to intervene between the front and the 'play' of the horse's shoulder. It will then be in its proper position.

All saddles and bridles should be kept scrupulously clean and soft by the use of the sponge and soap. White soap should be the only kind allowed for the purpose, and it should be well rubbed out with the stable-rubber after it has been rubbed in. The seat and panelling of the saddle should be kept well brushed, and all dust and scurf well beaten out, and every part of the saddle should receive proper attention.

No saddle composition, such as 'saddle paste,' should ever be used or allowed. They give, it is true, a brilliant polish to the leather, but they are nasty and sticky preparations, and grooms are ever apt to overdo it and put on too much. It is a capital thing for a lazy groom, who is able thereby to make a dirty saddle appear to be clean, and so it becomes but a means of glazing dirt. Moreover, these preparations ruin one's breeches, and it is well-nigh impossible to get the composition out of them.

I would caution the reader also, if he wears riding-boots of ordinary leather, and which are cleaned with blacking, to be careful to see that his servant is particular in removing any of the blacking which may rub off the boots on to the saddle-flaps, inasmuch as, if this is not observed, and he should use the saddle when wearing top or other boots, they will suffer very considerably and permanently.

With these remarks I will close this chapter; and I cannot think of anything which I have omitted to refer to which is likely to be of service to an ordinary person regarding the articles of which it treats.

The prices of saddles vary from five to six guineas ; side-saddles, from eleven guineas ; single snaffles, from 15s. complete ; double bridles, complete, from £1 5s.; girths, from 7s. 6d. to 15s.; breast-plates, from 12s. 6d. to £1.

CHAPTER XV.

Harness. — Parts of harness. — Headstall.—Bit. — Bridoon-hangers. — Buckles. — Harness furniture. — Metal brow-bands.—Evils of old-fashioned driving-bit.—' Liverpool ' bits.—Sliding ports.—Use of bit-bars.—Blinkers.—Crest-brushes. — Collars. — Hames. — Hames-rings. — Saddle-terrets.—Danger of bearing-rein hooks.—Back-band— Tugs.—Belly-band.—' Tilbury ' tugs.—Crupper.—Breeching.—Traces.—Spare traces.—Kicking-straps.—Reins.— Billets.—Use and abuse of bearing-reins.—Harness cleaning, black and brown.—Brasswork.—How to clean patent leather.—Harness-cleaning utensils and prices.—How to harness a horse to a carriage.—How to unharness a horse from a carriage.—Double harness.—Roller-bolts. --Uses of pole. — Pole-chains. — Coupling-reins. — Fitting of coupling-reins.—Carriages.—Horse and carriage to be suitably proportioned.—Care of carriages.—Varnish must be dry.—Abuse of the spoke-brush.—How to clean a carriage.—Water-hose.—Wheel-lift.—Use and abuse of wheel-lift.—Care of carriage-poles.—Care of wheels.— Tramway lines.—Evil effects of sun on a carriage.—List and prices of carriage-cleaning utensils.

As I devoted the last chapter to the consideration of saddles and saddlery, I propose to refer to that of harness in the present, its cleaning and preservation, also to the cleaning and preservation of carriages, and the utensils which are requisite for the above purposes.

A set of harness consists of many portions. I do not intend, neither do I consider it necessary, to enter into *minute* details, and it will suffice for the present purpose to treat only of what may be called the main portion. A set of harness consists of the following parts, viz. :

> Headstall and bit.
> Collar and hames : traces.
> Saddle, back-band and tugs.
> Crupper and breeching.
> Reins.
> Bearing-reins.
> Kicking-strap.

Harness headstalls are made on the same principle as those for use in saddle, with the addition of blinkers and a nose-band.

The bit consists of a bit and curb-chain only, unless where a horse is driven in a snaffle, when no bit is of course necessary. The bit or snaffle is also made to buckle on, and is not sewn on to the headstall.

Where a bearing-rein is used, a snaffle is also used with the bit, and for this purpose the headstall is provided with two metal rings for the rein of the bearing-bit to run through. These are called bridoon hangers, the rein being made round at this portion of its length for the purpose of allowing it to run freely and smoothly. A driving headstall is fitted on the horse in the same manner as that of an ordinary bridle. All harness buckles should be of plain metal, and *never* covered with leather. As I have before remarked, the metals generally used for this purpose are either brass or plated, or, in rare cases, silver. Brass harness, to my way of thinking, looks smarter and better than plated, is more easily cleaned, and wears better, but this is a matter of choice. It is certainly more generally used, and I may here remark that all harness furniture should be (save for the crests or monograms on the saddle and blinkers) as plain, light, and simple as possible, of smooth metal, and not one bit more of it used than is absolutely necessary. A metal browband is quite admissible for harness, but it should not be too elaborate. The metal browband is often sewn on to patent leather, but I do not think such an arrangement looks as well as the plain open links of the metal, and the latter is cooler, and quite as strong as is necessary. The old-fashioned driving-bits were made with a bar which connected the ends of the shanks of the bit, but these are now discarded, and rightly so, since they were dangerous, and horses were apt to get them under the shaft or pole.

The best pattern of driving-bit is what is known as the 'Liverpool.' The cheeks or shanks are separate, and the mouthpiece is made to move up and down, with a play of about an inch between its stops, forming what is called a 'sliding port.' Such sliding ports certainly cause a horse to 'play' on the bit, but I do not altogether like them, as I do not think they act quite as they should. They are all very well when a horse is standing still and 'mouthing' his bit, but when the rein is drawn tight, the mouthpiece *jumps*, as it were, and must be very much of a shock to the horse, and I prefer the use of a bit which does not slide.

A driving-bit has usually two slots pierced through the shank, so as to allow of the reins being fastened high or low, according as it may be desired to increase or decrease its power. These slots are termed the 'middle' and 'lower' bars. A horse may, therefore, be driven either from the ring which is level with the mouthpiece, and which is called the 'cheek,' the 'middle,' or the 'lower' bar; and it is a by no means uncommon thing to see a horse, especially in double harness, driven on the cheek on one side of the mouth, and the middle or lower bar on the other, but this, of course, is only resorted to where a horse, from either bad breaking or from being too constantly driven on one side of the pole in double harness, has one side of the mouth harder than the other.

Blinkers are used for the prevention of shying, and there are many horses which would not go quietly if they could see a carriage behind them, yet which are perfectly tractable in blinkers. Again, many a horse will shy when fresh, and the consequences of shying in harness are often very serious. Many people eschew the use of blinkers on the ground that they are useless. *This* they most certainly are *not*, although there are many horses which will go without them. Nevertheless, they *may* be useful and prevent an accident, and their appearance is also in their favour. A horse without blinkers in harness looks very plain and un-English-like. Blinkers are made either round or square. The latter have the smartest appearance. Where crests are worn on harness, it is necessary to use proper materials to clean them with, and shields and brushes are made on purpose, as without these the powder or brass-paste used to clean the metal with is very apt to soil the patent leather. The price of these brushes is about 2s. a pair.

Collars are usually made of patent leather. As the entire draught of a carriage is from these, it is

COLLARS. 157

necessary that they should fit the horse perfectly. Nearly every horse requires his own collar. Collar-making is a trade by itself. A good saddler will very readily fit a horse for a collar, and as they are made in many sizes, if he has not the proper size in stock, he can always obtain it in the course of a few hours. If a collar is too small or too large, a horse is sure to suffer. Of the two evils, the latter is the lesser. What are termed 'piped' collars should always have the preference.

The hames are two curved pieces of metal which fit round the collar, and to which the traces are attached. They are fastened on to the collar by means of a buckle and strap at the top, and by either a buckle and strap or a metal chain at the bottom. They should fit the fluting of the collar *exactly*. They should never, for the sake of appearance, be covered with leather. If the rest of the harness is brass, they should of course be of brass also, and *vice versâ*.

There are two rings on the hames for the reins to run through. These rings should never be made fixed or standing, but should always be folding. If standing, a rein might get twisted round them, and the most serious accident occur. Such has *many* a time been the case.

The rings, or terrets, as they are called, on the

driving saddle, should be round, and of no other shape. They are at times made square (if *rings* can be said to be *square*), but these are dangerous, and do not look well or workmanlike. These terrets, or, as the uninitiated frequently call them, turrets, are for the purpose of preventing the reins from falling on to the horse's sides, and catching in any part of the harness, etc. There is generally, in the centre of the saddle, an upright terret, to which the bearing-rein, when such is worn, is fixed. The upright pattern is better than a hook, as is sometimes used, the latter being very awkward and likely to damage the groom, as I have known to be the case, when the latter is fastening the bearing-rein, as if by chance a horse suddenly moves his head down at the time, the groom's finger or thumb (being between the hook and the rein) may possibly be driven on to the hook.

The back-band is made to run through the saddle, between its upper and lower leathers, *i.e.*, underneath its skirts. At either end of this back-band are the 'tugs,' as they are called, and these serve to support the shafts. The stops on the shafts also bear against these, and prevent the carriage running forward on to the horse. From the tugs is continued a broad, strong leather strap, called the belly-band, and this is used for the purpose of keeping the tugs and shafts down in their places, and also, in a two-wheeled carriage, it prevents the shafts from flying up when, any undue weight being placed on the hinder part of the carriage, the latter is thrown out of balance.

The belly-band should be fitted loosely, so as to allow free play to the shafts.

The 'Tilbury' tug is a great improvement on the old-fashioned loop-tug, because whereas in the latter the shafts require to be pushed *through*, in the former they can be at once laid in their places.

The crupper is fastened to a D in the cantle of the saddle, and there is a loop left between its leathers for the loin-strap of the breeching to pass through.

The breeching is used for the purpose of assisting the horse to keep the carriage back when going down hill, and is buckled on to the breeching-stops, which are fixed on the shafts for this purpose. When a horse is standing still on level ground the loin-straps of the breeching should hang straight down on both sides, the quarter-strap being well clear of the horse's quarters.

I need hardly make mention of the traces further than to remark that they must be as good of their kind as possible. It is a wise plan to carry a spare trace when driving. It may *never* be required, but if it should be it is *there*. This, perhaps, savours somewhat of the 'White Knight and his Mousetrap' in 'Alice in Wonderland'; but a broken trace may prove very awkward, and a trace may be broken or have to be cut should an accident happen.

A kicking-strap denotes its use by its very name, and is merely a strong broad strap, which, passing through the crupper, as does the breeching, is, like it, buckled to the shafts to stops placed there for the purpose. Where a horse is at all inclined to kick it should *always* be worn, as the breeching is not sufficient for the purpose.

Reins should be flat, and *never round*. Whether they are of brown or half brown and half black leather is immaterial, provided they are *good*. The all-brown perhaps *look* the better of the two; but in any case constant care is essential, in order that the ends which buckle on to the bit, the ' billets,' as they are called, are kept in proper repair, as the stitching of the billets is very apt to wear out—the saliva from the horse's mouth constantly wetting it; and it is generally at these points, or where the leather is worn thin by frequent rubbing against the terrets and collar-rings, that a rein breaks.

Of late years there has been a great deal said and written on the subject of bearing-reins, and their use is alleged to be a cruelty. Such doubtless is the case when they are improperly fitted, but where the reverse, I must say, I fail to see any more cruelty than there is in a bit. When a horse bores in harness they are almost a necessity, and are the greatest help to a coachman, especially when driving in a crowded thoroughfare. Of course, when a horse does not require a bearing-rein, it is as senseless to use one as it would be to use an umbrella in fine weather. It is not the *use* of the bearing-rein which is cruel, but rather its 'abuse.' All harness is cruel if it is badly fitted, and I venture to assert, judging from my own observation, that horses, as a general rule, suffer *far* more by reason of their throat-lashes being too tight than they would by even a somewhat *over-tight* bearing-rein. True, they should not suffer at all, nor can they from a bearing-rein which is properly fitted. From many years' experience in coach-driving, I can vouch for the assistance they offer to an aching arm at the end of a long stage with a heavy load and a boring wheeler. It has not been the fashion to use them in a coach for several years past; but I have often regretted the necessity of being obliged to eschew their use. So long as a horse can stretch his neck out sufficiently to draw his load, there can be no cruelty in their use, and when he takes to going 'on his shoulders,' at the expense of the muscles of the driver's arm, he is all the better for a lightly fitted bearing-rein.

Black harness is best cleaned with the harness composition sold for the purpose.

Brown harness may be cleaned with soap, like an ordinary saddle. A *very* little saddle-paste may be allowed on brown harness.

The brass of harness is best cleaned with the brillantine sold for the purpose, and it retains its polish longer than by the use of any other preparation with which I am acquainted.

Patent leather will look better and last longer if cleaned in the following way, viz. : Sponge it with warm (not too hot) water and quickly dry it; then, while still warm, rub a very little sweet-oil into it, rub it out again, and finish with a leather. This recipe was given me very many years ago by a first-class coachbuilder, as being the best way to clean patent leather, and I have since then never used anything else, whether for the patent leather on a carriage-harness or for boots. The oil must, however, be *well* rubbed out again. I only know one thing against this recipe, and that is its simplicity. Most people prefer to buy a bottle of so-called polishing cream. The latter is very good in its way, I have no doubt, and, indeed, I am aware that it is excellent, but I prefer the recipe I have given.

The utensils required for cleaning harness are:

	s.	d.
1 compo-brush, about . . .	1	6
1 set of crest-brushes . . .	2	0
1 bit-brush	1	0
	4	6

harness-paste, oil, brillantine, chamois leathers, rubbers, etc.

What I have before remarked regarding the preservation of saddlery applies equally to harness.

How to harness a Horse to a Carriage.

Fit the shafts into the tugs.

Fasten the traces.

Fasten the belly-band.

Fasten the breeching-straps.

Untie the reins, and having placed them between the thumb and forefinger, and the *second* and *third* fingers of the left hand, the near-side rein being that between the two first-named, you can mount the box; but make it a golden rule never to mount or dismount from the box of a carriage without your reins, and never allow anyone to get into a carriage until the driver is mounted on the box.

To UNHARNESS A HORSE FROM A CARRIAGE.

Double up the reins neatly and pass them through the terret-rings on the saddle, and tie them there.

Unfasten the belly-band.

Unfasten the breeching.

Unfasten the traces,
coiling both the belly-band and the traces neatly and securely. Remove the shafts from the tugs.

It will be observed that the first operation in 'putting to,' and the last in 'taking out,' is the fastening and unfastening of the traces, and for this reason: unless the traces are fastened before anything else in putting to, should the horse start off, the tugs or breeching would probably be broken. Inversely, for the same reason, they should be left on till the last.

Double harness is made on precisely the same principle as single, with the exception that, there being no shafts, no shaft-tugs are required, the steering of the carriage being effected by means of the pole.

The draught of the carriage is from the splinter-bar direct, on which are placed roller-bolts, to which the traces are affixed. As there are no shafts or tugs, there is, consequently, no breeching which can serve to keep back the carriage as in single harness. The carriage is therefore kept back by the horses drawing *against* the pole. In order to effect this, there is connection between the pole and the horses by means of pole-straps or pole-chains, which latter, being fastened to the end of the pole, are passed through a ring with which the hames are furnished, and drawn up just tight enough to allow a fairly backward and forward play of the horse. The pole also is made so as to play *slightly* up and down in its socket. The great point to be attended to in fastening the pole-chains is to allow just sufficient play, and no more, as too much or too little might tend to spring or, worse still, break the pole.

The arrangement of the reins in double harness is necessarily different from that for single. The number of reins in the hand of the driver is the same, but each rein is *split* or divided at about half its length. These act as follows: The upper (as it is held in the hand) rein, or, as it may be called for simplicity, the near-side or left rein, is buckled to the near side of the near horse's bit, and the near side of the off horse's bit; therefore if that rein is pulled both horses are made to turn to the left. The off or right rein is similarly fastened to the bits of the horses on the off side of their bits, so that when this is pulled both horses turn to the right. The two inner reins (the couplers, as they are called) necessarily, therefore, cross each other between the horses. Where they cross it is customary to use a metal or bone ring to connect them. The reins at the couplings are provided with a running buckle and strap, so as to admit of the coupling-reins being lengthened or shortened as desired.

In harnessing horses for double harness, it is of consequence that these coupling-reins should be of such a length that each horse is kept *straight* to his work and neither bears away from nor cuddles the pole, as also that each horse is poled up by means of the pole-chains, so as to further ensure, as far as can be, his being in the best position to do his fair share of work.

Carriages.

A gentleman's carriage can hardly be too simple and plain, whether in shape or colour, or too good as far as its material and workmanship are concerned. If the carriage, therefore, is good of its kind, the horses should also be good and suitable for that carriage—suitable in size and class; their colour is immaterial. Nothing looks worse than a good carriage and a bad horse; the good workmanship of the former attracts attention to the want of good quality in the latter. A large carriage drawn by a small horse is equally out of keeping, as is also the reverse: the whole affair is out of balance. But it is a very common occurrence to see horses harnessed to a carriage which is far too large and heavy for their powers. Such is not economy, either, inasmuch as the horse under these conditions must wear out sooner.

A carriage is not kept in good order without great care and labour. We will consider how this may be expended to the best advantage.

In the first place, as I have before remarked, the coach-house must be dry and suitable. The carriage itself must also be dry. The reader may remark, 'What on earth do you mean by the carriage being dry?' I refer to the painting and varnishing when a carriage is handed over from the builder, for carriages are far too often brought into use before they are fit to be used. All paint and varnish should be allowed a reasonable time to dry and harden thoroughly before being exposed to wear. Where this is not done the lustre of the varnish soon goes, and then the varnish itself follows suit, and the result is that the paint, being unprotected, also suffers; and lastly, in extreme cases, the wood, being exposed to wet and damp, gets rotten, and the carriage is ruined. It is therefore necessary to allow a due period to elapse between the time a carriage is finished and the time it is brought into use.

A careless servant will in a very short time knock a carriage about and effect through his rough handling in cleaning more damage in a fortnight than should be caused by years of fair wear. The wheels, being the most difficult portions to clean, are generally the first to suffer. As a rule, the spoke-brush is the weapon which inflicts the most serious wounds; for as it is worked between the spokes of the wheel, unless care is exercised in its use, the back, striking against the opposite spoke, knocks the paint off it. Who that keeps a carriage is not familiar with the 'tap, tap, tapping' of the back of the spoke-brush against the wheels? Of course, a good servant will not be guilty of this castanet accompaniment.

We will suppose that a carriage has just come in dirty. As soon as possible, if daylight permits, it should be cleaned. No mud should ever be allowed to remain on all night if it is *possible* to remove it; the lime, etc., off the roads tend, if left, to destroy the varnish. All mud, therefore, should be sluiced off with water, and these sluicings should be repeated until every speck of mud has been *washed* off. When this has been done, the water may be removed by the use of a sponge, the greatest care being exercised that no grit which may be taken up by the sponge is rubbed over the varnish, as it will most assuredly scratch it and leave a permanent mark. When the water has thus been sponged off, a leather may be used to finish up with, and when everything is *quite* dry, a fresh dry leather may be lightly passed over. In the washing the under parts of the carriage must receive as much attention as the rest. The cushions having been removed and thoroughly dusted, and the inside lining brushed, the metal work may be cleaned, and the work is completed.

The carriage may then be placed in the coach-house, and should be completely covered with a linen cover, in order to preserve it from dust, etc.

Where possible, a hose will be found of the greatest service in cleaning carriages; but it is essential, in any case, that the ground whereon the carriage is placed for washing should be paved, inasmuch as, if this is not observed, the splashings from the gravel prevent the wheels from being properly finished. If it is impossible to finish a carriage the same day that it is used, the washing should never be omitted.

I never allow the use of a spoke-brush on the wheels of a carriage, and would, if I could, abandon its use altogether; but there are parts of the under-carriage which cannot be well reached without its use, and so I look upon it as a necessary evil.

It is necessary to use what is termed a wheel-set or wheel-lift for cleaning the wheels. This is no more than a lever on a stand, which, being placed under the end of the axle, lifts the wheel off the ground, so as to allow of its being turned round while being cleaned; but the wheel should never be so lifted one bit more than is absolutely necessary to allow it to just clear the ground, otherwise the carriage may be strained.

A carriage-pole when not in use should, if possible, be kept in an upright position, and a rack should be provided for this purpose, in order that it may not get 'set,' or bent out of shape; for too often poles are hung up on racks, and the result is that they acquire a twist, and of course are then more liable to break.

The wheels of carriages which are much used require to be kept constantly looked to and oiled, and the 'washers,' as they are called, renewed as often as they become worn. A few shillings thus expended will often save several pounds. Every carriage should have its wheels examined at *least* once a quarter, and, where the work is constant, once a month.

Nowadays, when tramways are met with in every town of any size, the wheels of carriages suffer a great deal of damage, and care is necessary to prevent their running in the lines of tramways, when the horse, pulling in an opposite direction, must give a severe wrench to them. A good coachman will be careful to avoid this, and to cross the lines of rail at such an angle that the wheels of his carriage cannot get into them. A careless one will twist every wheel and spring every bolt in no time, much, perhaps, to the benefit of the coach-builder.

A hot sun is very detrimental to the varnish of a carriage; strange to say, a spring sun is the worst of all. Therefore, a carriage should never be left standing in the sun if shade is available.

The utensils required for cleaning a carriage, and their prices, are as follow:

	£	s.	d.
1 wheel-lift (iron)	0	10	6
1 spoke-brush	0	6	0
1 cloth carriage ditto	0	5	0
2 medium sized sponges	0	4	0
2 chamois leathers	0	4	0
3 rubbers	0	1	6
	1	11	0

PART III.
FEEDING AND FARRIERY.

CHAPTER XVI.

Forage.—Hay.—Average price of hay.—Weight of hay.—Meadow-hay.—Old v. new hay.—Selection of hay.—Perfect hay.—Mow-burnt hay.—How to test quality of hay. — Rye-grass and clover. — Oats. — English and foreign oats.—Black, white, and gray oats.—Weight of oats.—Testing weight of oats. — Price of oats. — Old oats. —Made-up oats.—How to detect made-up oats.—How to select oats.—Weighing oats.—Straw.—Varieties of straw.—Foreign competition.—Price of straw.—Oat-straw. — Bedding. — Fern. — Sawdust. — Peat-mould. — Moss-litter.—Bran.—Price of bran.

The subject of forage, which I am now about to treat of, may, I think, with advantage be divided into three separate portions, which we will, for the sake of convenience, classify under the following headings, viz. : ordinary, extra, and green forage. These can again be subdivided as required.

Under the head of ordinary forage I include the following, viz. : hay, oats, straw, and bran, and we will therefore take them in that order.

Hay, such as is fit for food for horses, is of two kinds, viz. : natural (or that which grows naturally) and artificial (or that which is sown annually). We will assume that the prices of the two kinds are the same, as such assumption is sufficiently accurate for our purpose.

The price of hay is dependent on the season, as may be inferred, a bad season raising the price very considerably, at times doubling the ordinary price, a good season having a nearly corresponding effect. One season taken with another, over a term of years, gives as a good average price, for good sound hay, of about £5 a ton.

I will here remark for the benefit of the reader, as well as to facilitate any further remarks on the subject of feeding, etc., that hay, being cut into trusses, as is the general, if not universal, custom in England, runs forty trusses to the ton weight, and each truss is reckoned to weigh 56 lb., giving thereby the full complement of 2,240 lb. to the ton.

The hay which is the most suitable for riding-horses, or horses which have to travel fast, is undoubtedly natural hay. This should be as good and sound as can be obtained, and no hay should be used in a gentleman's stable before the close of the year in which it has been cut. Thus, hay which has been cut in June should never be used *before* the 1st January following. Even then it is more advisable to use that of the previous season, if procurable, and *good*; but if *not* good, then it is better to use that of a later crop, should it be superior. *Nothing* is more harmful to horses, and nothing more wasteful, than bad hay.

It may be asked, 'But how is good hay distinguished from bad?'

I would strongly advise the reader, if he has the opportunity, to enlist the services of some friend or person who is competent to instruct him, and get him to show him, by a visit to the nearest haymarket, how to discriminate between the two. It is a very simple thing to learn, and an hour or two thus spent will teach him sooner and better than *I* can hope to do by means of my pen alone. Nevertheless, I will endeavour to explain as simply and clearly as I can, and if my explanation should not prove sufficient, it will at all events be a *little* knowledge, and *not* 'a dangerous thing,' for a little knowledge of the subject is better than none at all.

1. Hay should be of a good colour, as nearly as possible of the colour it was when first stacked; and this colour should be general all through the rick.

2. It should have a good mixture of grasses in it, and be free from thistles and any coarser growths.

3. There should be a fair sprinkling of flowers

in it, and the colour of these flowers, the yellow ones especially, should be fresh, and but little different from what they were when growing.

4. It should be sweet and fragrant, and be absolutely free from any sour or acrid smell.

5. It should be soft and silky in texture, and fairly long.

6. It should not be too brittle or dusty.

Such is the description of what perfect upland hay should be, and where such is obtainable a good price should not be grudged for it; and if it is possible to buy a rick of it at a time, it will be money well spent, as any overplus will *always* command a good price.

Coarser hay than that described above is better adapted for food, if well saved, than a finer quality which is yellow or sour.

Hay which has been too quickly stacked, or which has been put up wet, is certain to become what is termed 'mow-burnt.' A rick of such hay will, when cut, appear of a very brown colour, and will probably be here and there blotched with very dark, almost black, seams running through the rick in various places, showing how intense the heat must have been, and how very nearly the rick has been on fire through its becoming over-heated. Hay from such ricks always has an over-sweet—

indeed, sickly—smell, and there are many people who, knowing no better, are led to suppose that *because* of this sweet smell such hay is necessarily very good. Horses will eat it greedily, and so their idea gains ground; but such hay is not fit for food for horses at all, is most injurious, and affects their kidneys, and may, if given as food for any lengthened period, cause disease. A very little common-sense exercised in the selection of hay will suffice, if not to secure *good* hay, at all events to prevent the purchase of *very* bad.

Let the reader take up a handful of hay and examine it. He will, at all events, be able to see for himself if there is a *variety* of grasses in it, or if they are all alike, and it is quite possible that he may be able to recognise some of the grasses, and if so, he may be still further able to pronounce whether they are those which grow on good or poor land. Poor land will not as a rule produce good hay; inversely, good grasses will not grow on poor land. I do not mean to infer, of course, that poor land may not be *made* fruitful by manures and dressings, etc., but by 'poor land' I mean land which was in a poor condition when the grass was growing on it.

So much for natural hay. We will now turn to the consideration of artificial hay, and we need not for our purpose make mention of more than the two following, viz.: rye-grass and clover. Rye-grass is often sown alone; clover, for hay, generally in conjunction with rye-grass.

Rye-grass will be readily recognised when I describe it as being the grass with which children play at soldier, sailor, etc.

Clover everyone knows by sight as well as by name, and though there are several varieties of it, it will be enough for us to treat them all as one.

Rye-grass is a strong, nutritious grass, and, when well saved, a very valuable hay.

It is perhaps, as is clover, somewhat over-strong for galloping horses (hunters and such-like), excepting as a change, for a short time, to ordinary upland hay. It is, however, a crop which requires careful making, and should be very good of its kind. Its colour, when cut from the rick, is often of a pale yellow; but in all other respects, as far as smell and regularity of colour are concerned, the remarks which I have made with reference to natural hay hold good in its selection. Clover is perhaps the most difficult of the three to save well. Its leaves turn *very* dark when dried, but the flowers in the rick should wear a full share of colours. It necessarily makes a coarse hay, and, as such, mixes well with rye-grass. I, however, prefer the use of upland hay for ordinary purposes. Rye-grass, or rye-grass mixed with clover, is not ill adapted for carriage work, but, as I before remarked, it should not be given for too long a period without change to the lighter, natural hay.

We may divide oats into two classes—viz., English and foreign. Time was when the latter were well-nigh unknown in the home markets. Of late years, however, foreign competition has done its best to drive home produce altogether out of the field, and foreign oats can now be bought at prices at which the British farmer cannot grow them, to obtain anything like a profit. These foreign oats, too, are, as a rule, very good. They may not be quite as heavy as some of our best English, but they are good enough for all ordinary purposes, and, as I say, their price is also in their favour.

Oats are either white, black, or gray. The foreign oats are either white or black, more generally the latter, and whether English or foreign, I must confess that I am prejudiced in favour of black, inasmuch as, although they may not have so plump and full an appearance as the white, their skins are generally thinner, and the quantity of actual food in them is certainly greater, comparatively speaking. Perhaps the best variety of all is the gray oat; but such are more expensive, and not always to be readily procured. They are, of course, in the market, but they are, as a rule, grown for home consumption.

Oats are sold very generally over England by the 'quarter,' as it is termed. A quarter consists of two sacks, and a sack consists of four bushels. A bushel of oats should weigh not *less* than 38 lb., exclusive, of course, of the weight of the bushel-measure. In order to test the weight of oats, adopt the following plan : First carefully weigh the empty bushel-measure, then fill it with oats as rapidly as possible, brush off the oats level with the top of the measure by means of a flat stick turned edgewise (a broom-handle will answer the purpose), and weigh the measure full. Subtract the weight of the empty measure from the full weight, and the result will give you the number of pounds to the bushel. Oats weighing 38 lb. to the bushel may be considered as fair, 40 lb. as good, and all above that as very good. There are varieties of oats which come into the market at weights *very considerably* in excess of 40 lb. to the bushel, such as some of the Scotch and Irish varieties ; but these are not to be bought except at high prices. Of course, the heavier the oat the better, provided that the skins are not unduly thick. Good honest oats of 38 lb. to 39 lb. to the bushel may be bought from the dealers for prices varying, according to the rise and fall of the market, from 14s. to £1 per quarter. Of course, when a large quantity is bought at a time, the price will be somewhat lessened. I myself was able, two years ago, through a friend, who had bought a large quantity, to buy some few quarters of good black oats weighing 42 lb. per bushel, at £1 per quarter. Oats, like hay, should never be used before the end of the year in which they have been grown, and a second-year oat is better than a last season one.

Corn-dealers are great adepts in making up oats for the market, and in bleaching and drying them if they have become damaged. If any doubt exists as to their having been dried in the kiln for bleaching purposes, it may be easily set at rest by rubbing some of the oats quickly between the palms of the hands, when the smell of the sulphur which is used in the kiln to bleach them will be noticeable on the hands. Oats which have been kiln-dried, even if not bleached, shrink unduly from the points of the husks, and so can very readily be detected, and they have a brown appearance at the points also.

In selecting oats, first smell them to ascertain if they are musty; then strip a few and examine them, and test them by pinching them with the nails. They should be crisp and floury. Finally, take some and chew them. They should have a pure, fresh, milky taste. If such oats are a proper weight, you may safely buy them, provided they can stand the above tests.

In weighing oats, *insist* that the bushel-measure is filled quickly. A sharp, dishonest dealer will, by slowly filling and shaking the measure, apparently accidentally, make oats weigh some two or three pounds more to the bushel than is their fair, actual weight. Taking oats of 40 lb. to the bushel as a fair sample, it will be seen that each sack should weigh 160 lb. At 38 lb. it would weigh 152 lb.

The use of straw in a stable is restricted principally to that for bedding purposes. Good wheat-straw is the best, and the better it is of its kind the longer it will last; consequently, it is true economy to ever buy the best which can be procured. Where wheat-straw is not easily to be obtained, oat-straw may be substituted for it; but it is very inferior, and does not last as long or look so well as wheat.

The price of straw varies very considerably, according as the season has been good or bad. Of late years the price has been generally higher, and it will, I fear, rise still more, inasmuch as the farmers, finding that it does not pay them to grow wheat to the same extent as formerly, are, as far as it is possible, giving up very much of their arable land and turning it into pasture. Moreover, so many farms are now unlet, and there is so much land in the country absolutely uncultivated, or at least but imperfectly worked, that our wheat-growing is at a low ebb at present. Foreign competition is of course the cause. I have read that the country which has the command of corn is the strongest Power, and I can readily understand the writer's meaning when he asserts such to be the case. So long as we *have* the command of the sea, so long we can retain our power; the instant we lose that, we are doomed. 'Have we that command?' is a question continually put before the public. It seems by no means too certain that we have. Goodness only knows what will become of the country if, losing that command, our foreign supplies are cut off from us. It is too unpleasant a thought for us to dwell on here. Taking one part of the country with another, the present price of straw appears, as far as I can ascertain, to be from 55s. to 60s. per ton. The latter is the better price to allow for its cost. There are, of course, districts where corn is not much grown, in which this price is considerably exceeded.

Oat-straw does very fairly well when used as chaff, but chaff is more suitable for carriage horses and such-like work, except in special cases.

It is difficult to know what to use as a substitute for straw for bedding purposes. Fern is not good, as it harbours ticks. Still, it is perhaps the next best substitute. Sawdust is perhaps even better than fern, but it should be beech, and not deal or oak, inasmuch as the resin in the one, and the tannin in the other, is bad for the feet, and is apt to render them brittle.

Peat-mould, well dried and sifted, will answer very well for use during the summer, but it requires constant care and raking over, and *looks* comfortless.

The moss-litter, which is so much used, has many advantages and many disadvantages, and I hardly know whether to praise it or condemn it. It is very handy, inasmuch as, being sold in compressed bundles, a large supply occupies but a small space. It is cheaper than straw. Horses' feet do well on it, and the horn is kept tough and sound. This I have proved to be the case. So far, I have nothing to say against it, but horses *do* eat it, and it *must* be harmful to them; moreover, it is the most dreadful stuff to use in a stable, as, without the *greatest* care being exercised, it very soon stops up the drains, and so is a source of constant expense and inconvenience. The smaller particles get washed down with the water, and, settling in the drains, swell, and so block them. Apart from these objections, which may certainly be guarded against, I have no reason for condemning its use, or pronouncing it to be otherwise than excellent, save for its appearance.

There is but little to remark with regard to bran, further than that it should be fresh, and for this reason it is always better to purchase only a small quantity at a time. Musty or dirty bran should never be used, not even for a poultice; it is better thrown away. Its average price is about 1s. a bushel. Where possible, it is better when obtained direct from the mill, as it is more likely to be fresh.

CHAPTER XVII.

Extra forage.—Beans.—Price of beans.—Quantity and effects of beans.—Peas.—Price of peas.—Maize.—Use of maize.—Price of maize.—Linseed.—Linseed-mashes.—Merits of linseed mashes.—Linseed-oil.—Cooked foods.—Advantages of cooked foods.—Effects of cooked foods.—Preparation of cooked foods.—Green forage.—Quantity of green forage to be given.—Lucerne.—Carrots.—Price of carrots.—Quantity of food required for a horse.—Daily scale of food.—Cost of horse-keep.—Annual cost of horse-keep.—Feeding horses.—Chaff.—Indigestion.—Hay and straw for chaff.—Feeding-hours.—Feeding with hay.—Watering.—Food and work.—Bad feeders.—Instinct.—Coaxing delicate feeders.—Mice in stable.—Rock-salt.—Bran-mashes.—How to make bran-mashes.—Bran-poultices.—Linseed-poultices.—How to make linseed-poultices.—Gruel.—How to make gruel.—Ale for tired horse.—An English sportsman.

UNDER the head of what we have decided to call 'extra forage' may be reckoned the following—viz., beans, peas, maize, linseed, oatmeal.

Beans, as given for food for horses, should never be *less* than a year old. They are generally used for the purpose crushed, and it is therefore very easy to ascertain their condition; suffice it to say that they should be hard, and not soft. Old beans in good condition are *very* hard. Beans are usually sold by the bushel. The price of good old beans is about 5s. 6d. per bushel. As food for horses, they must be used with discretion. They are stimulating, and are heating, and there are many horses which cannot stand them. They should at no time be given for a lengthened period, as they are apt to induce swelled legs, humours, and itchiness of the skin. A double-handful is an ample quantity for an ordinary horse. I may add that their use is by no means as general as it was formerly, and I think it is as well, for much harm was produced from a too liberal diet of them.

Peas possess all the advantageous properties of beans without their detrimental qualities, and where such food is required, it is better to use them in preference to beans; but these also should be given in moderation (much the same in quantity as beans), and their use should not be over-long continued. The *white* peas are best suited for horses. They are somewhat expensive as horse-food, but they are a good addition at times, and put heart into, and muscle on, a weakly horse. Their price is about 5s. 6d. per bushel.

Maize, or Indian corn, is hardly suitable for horses which are used for fast work. For slow carriage work, and for big, heavy draught horses, it answers very well. I am given to understand that it is much used in the large tram and omnibus-stables, and is, I have no doubt, excellent for such a purpose; but it is over-strong as food for a gentleman's stable. I have no doubt but that, when properly cooked, it would answer well for carriage-horses. Its price is about 4s. per bushel.

Linseed is a most valuable addition to the stable *menu*. It is used for mashes, and is, where a horse will eat it, a most desirable article of food, especially after a hard day's work, such as hunting. It requires long and careful cooking, until it is like a jelly. Therefore, when a horse leaves the stable on a hunting day, his linseed-mash may be at once set on to cook, and it will not be ready any too soon for him, whatever time he may come in.

The merit of linseed lies chiefly in the fact that, whereas it is a laxative, gentle and soothing, its use by no means weakens the strength of a horse, its laxative powers being more than compensated for by its nutritious qualities. Used as a meal, it is invaluable for the purposes of poulticing. In the form of oil, it is equally useful in other ways as a tonic and flesh-former; but I will refer to its use in these two forms later on.

I think it is Mr. Mayhew who, in his book on

the horse, advocates the use of cooked foods. Some years ago I tried them on a mare which I could not get into as good condition as I wished, and I can certainly, and with the greatest confidence, speak to the very excellent results which followed the adoption of his advice. Never was a change more rapidly or completely effected for the better. She at once began putting on good firm flesh, and certainly no horse could have possibly been more fit to go, or looked in higher condition, than she did in the course of a very few weeks, and she carried me brilliantly through the rest of the season. Despite this fitness, her dung was always loose—so much so as to be an annoyance, especially in the hunting field. I did not, therefore, continue its use, although convinced of its efficiency. I prepared it in the following way in a very large fish-kettle, which I had constructed for the purpose, viz.: nearly all her food for the following day was put into the kettle, and *boiling* water poured over it in just sufficient quantity as to be completely absorbed, and the whole wrapped round with a couple of rugs. Whatever was left over was thrown away, so as to prevent its becoming stale (and such a preparation very quickly ferments), and fresh substituted. The reader can of course try this plan for himself if he has need of it. I only give him my own experience, and from its results express my belief in its use, as I am in honesty bound to do.

Green Forage.

What may be called 'green forage' may also include the following—viz., grass crops—carrots, lucerne, etc.

All kinds of young crops are used for green forage, and can in the season be bought by the bundle, varying in price. It is essential that it should be cut fresh daily, and it should be used in moderation. It becomes an excellent alterative for horses, and they eat it all too ravenously. Given in excess, it is dangerous, being mostly too laxative, and likely to produce colic, etc. It should be mixed carefully with the hay, and forked about well with it. A double-handful (and not too large a one) is quite enough when mixed with each feed of hay. It is, when thus properly used, a pleasant and beneficial change to the ordinary diet of a horse, and as much so as salad is to mankind.

Lucerne is but little grown in this country. I could wish it were more generally so than is the case, as it is most valuable as a green food, especially for horses. In India everyone who can grows it for his stable use, and it is a crop which will bear repeated cuttings. I do not mean to assert that lucerne could be used in this country as freely and generally as in India, or that its growth could be exactly similar, but it is nevertheless a valuable crop anywhere where it can be grown. I believe that it is an expensive one, and hence perhaps the reason why one so seldom sees it in this country. Wherever it *is* grown, however, it appears to thrive well.

Carrots are most useful to give to horses—two or three a day are sufficient. These should always be cut lengthwise, otherwise a horse may choke. The white variety are, I think, to be preferred to the red, when obtainable. They much assist horses in shedding their coats, but must not be used in immoderate quantity. The average price of horse carrots is about 40s. per ton; but is of course variable.

The reader will, perhaps, be anxious to learn what quantity of food is necessary for the well-doing of an ordinary horse, and I propose therefore to give him a scale to go by, which he can increase or diminish according as he may find necessary, and I think that I can hardly make use of a better one than that which is used in our cavalry. I have myself always found it sufficient for a horse of ordinary size.

I suppose that 15 hands 2 inches is the *average* height of our horses, and we shall do well, therefore, in the present instance to take that as our standard. I will here remark, for the benefit of the unlearned in such matters, that the height of a horse is reckoned by hands, and that each hand measures four inches; a horse, therefore, of 15.2 will be 62 inches high, or, in other words, 5 feet 2 inches.

The cavalry allowance for a horse of this height is reckoned as follows: Hay, 12 lb., oats, 10 lb., straw, 8 lb., per diem.

At first this allowance of straw is not sufficient, but after a few days, a fair bed having been made up, it will be found enough, especially if care is taken that only the *worst* of the soiled litter is thrown on to the manure-heap, and the rest is well dried daily. For horses doing hard, fast work the allowance of oats may be increased, the hay being decreased—the one very much balancing the other; and on this allowance, if the hay and corn are good of their kinds, a horse should do remarkably well. If he does *not*, it will be either because he is amiss or the groom is dishonest.

From the above scale the actual cost of keeping a horse can be arrived at, so that the reader can tell exactly what his stable expenses for ordinary forage ought *not* to exceed.

At the rate of 12 lb. per diem, a horse consumes some 79 trusses of hay per annum. As 40 trusses go to the ton, we will call it 80 trusses for simplicity of calculation. He therefore consumes two tons of hay annually, and this, being reckoned at £5 per ton, will give a total for hay of £10 annually.

Allowing oats to weigh 40 lb. to the bushel, each sack, therefore, weighing 160 lb., he will, at the rate of 10 lb. per diem, consume about $11\frac{1}{2}$ quarters (*i.e.*, 23 sacks) per annum. Reckoning the price of oats to be £1 per quarter, the annual cost will be £11 10s. With straw at £3 per ton, and an allowance of 8 lb. per diem, he will consume about one and a third tons annually, which will give a cost of £4.

Allowing a bushel of bran every month, which is a very good allowance, and the price of it to be 1s. per bushel, one gets the following figures, which represent the annual cost for ordinary forage, viz.:

	£	s.	d.
Hay	10	0	0
Oats	11	10	0
Straw	4	0	0
Bran	0	12	0
	26	2	0

It will be seen, therefore, that the cost of the actual food for a horse is *not* very great, or nearly as heavy as people are apt to imagine, and this, set against the cost of hiring, would probably show a balance the right way, and with good management it ought to do so, and a very good balance too, inasmuch as every horse should at least earn his keep. If he were *not* to do so, it would, indeed, be a poor look-out for livery-stable-keepers, and these latter invariably feed their horses well.

Ordinary horses are fed three times a day, viz. : in the morning, at mid-day, and in the evening ; but those which are delicate feeders may have their food divided into four, or even six, different feeds. No food which is left should ever be permitted to remain, but be taken away as soon as possible. Hay and corn are generally used as food, and these are given separately, of course. It is a good plan where a horse is a gross feeder and bolts his food, or where it is difficult to put flesh on a horse, to give chaff instead of hay alone.

Chaff is merely hay and straw mixed together and chopped up in a chaff-cutter, into lengths of about an inch. The corn and chaff may then be mixed together in a sieve and given to the horse, but it is necessary that they *should* be well mixed together, and well for the master to examine the manger now and again and see this *is* done ; for slight as the trouble is, grooms are very apt to neglect this mixing, and the entire object for which the chaff is given is defeated. As many horses are thin from indigestion as from other causes, especially in gentlemen's stables, where horses are apt to be overfed; and the result of indigestion is very often broken-wind, and all sorts of other ailments. The giving of chaff very much prevents this, and a greedy feeder—and such horses are very liable to get indigestion and become broken-winded—cannot bolt his corn if it is properly mixed with chaff. About one-third of straw to two of hay is a good proportion for chaff, but it must be borne in mind that both hay and straw must be good of their kind, and no refuse of either ever allowed to go into the chaff-cutter. I fear that the latter is very often used for cutting up rubbish which should never be given at all, and it is, indeed, an unfair and dirty trick to cheat the animal which works well and honestly of his well-earned food.

The hours for feeding horses in this country are generally as follows. It will be seen that watering invariably precedes feeding. The reason for this routine being observed I will give further on.

6 A.M. : Water and feed with a little hay.
7 A.M. : Feed with corn.
12 MID-DAY : Water and hay as before.
1 P.M. : Feed with corn.
5.30 P.M. : Water and hay.
6.30 P.M. : Feed with corn.

The hay should be divided so that the greater portion remains for the night's feed. It is better, if a horse is going out for work, that he should have the lesser quantity of hay, inasmuch as his wind will be the clearer for it. He may have as much corn as he will eat, in moderation; but his hay should be somewhat stinted. Indeed, for hunters, very little hay is required compared with other horses, and so their corn may be well increased. It is, however, always a good plan to let a horse have a lock or two of hay when fasting, as the stomach, being empty, is thereby better prepared for the feed of corn which is to follow. The greater quantity of hay may be well given at night, inasmuch as there are several hours which must necessarily elapse between the last feed at night and the first in the morning; and it is not natural for a horse to fast for many hours.

As regards the watering of horses *before* feeding, the reason is a very simple one, and it is this: A horse has two stomachs, or, I should say, what is equivalent to two stomachs. All fluid is carried through the first, or food stomach, into the second, or what answers the purpose of a second, viz., the cæcum, or blind gut. Now, if the corn is given first, *before* watering, the water must necessarily pass through the corn in its passage to the cæcum.

As is well known, the effect of water on corn is to swell the latter. Therefore, whether chewed or not, the result of water passing through the corn must be to swell it, and if the water is given *after* the corn, the latter, being swollen, may possibly cause colic—indeed, very frequently *does* so. If, however, the *reverse* system is adopted, the water, which at *once* passes on, is out of the way and can do no harm. A horse may be fed almost *immediately* after being watered with impunity; but at least an hour should elapse before watering if he has first been fed. It is a good plan, where a horse is kept in a loose-box, to let a bucket of water stand in the corner of the box, care being taken that the water is *constantly* changed. A horse will then drink when he requires it, and in smaller quantities at a time. A horse suffers very much from being kept unduly long without water —far more so than if kept without food. I have heard it stated that a forty-eight hours' abstinence from water will tame the most vicious horse. Therefore it especially behoves grooms, whose horses are in stalls where they cannot drink as they desire, to be early risers, and punctual to their time, in order that their horses may receive their allowance of water at the proper hour. In feeding horses the great thing to be observed is that their food and work are proportionate. A horse doing a great deal of hard work requires a proper proportion of hard food. Some horses, hunters especially, are very frequently so nervously constituted that they will not feed well, and the worst of it is that it is at the very times when they *should* get the food inside them, they refuse to eat. Such horses will often refuse their corn after the excitement of a day's hunting, and, what is almost as bad, will not feed before starting. They seem to know by instinct that they are going out. It is well-nigh impossible to cheat them. Animals are endowed with an instinct which is beyond our reasoning powers. Cavalry horses know the time better than the barrack clock, though I am free to admit that it is small blame to them if they do, since a barrack clock is generally about as bad a timekeeper as can be found. But even if the clock *be* wrong, they are not. When their feeding-time approaches, although there may have been no indication of it given, there is such a neighing, and screaming, and kicking, as if they were all mad. I could, of course, quote ever so many instances in proof of the sagacity of horses, but I will refrain from doing so, and return to what I was saying. It is, as I observed, very often a difficult matter to get an excitable horse to feed.

When such is the case, he must be coaxed into feeding. Some such horses will feed from the hand a little at a time. Most horses can be tempted by sugar, and a little brown sugar sprinkled over the corn will often have the desired effect. If not, the food must be taken away and offered again and again till the last thing at night, and then if still refused, it may be left in the manger in hopes that it may be taken in the night. I may here mention that mice in the stable are often the cause of horses not feeding. They get into the mangers and frighten the horses. The remedy is, of course, a simple one, viz. : a good stable cat.

Rock-salt should be kept in every manger. It has a most beneficial effect on the tone of a horse's stomach, and horses are very fond of it. It is *very* cheap (about 1d. per lb.), and a lump lasts a long time, as the horse only licks it and rolls it about.

I have known horses in India eat away at the stable walls and mangers, which are generally made of mud bricks dried in the sun, to get the saltpetre which is universally present in an Indian soil.

Where a horse is not doing much work, his food, as I have remarked, must be proportionate; he must have less hard food. Therefore, from one-third to one-half of his food may be made up of bran.

It is a wise plan to give every horse a bran-mash once a week; Saturday night seems the best, and is the general time for giving it. It is a laxative, and saves many a dose of physic. It is a plan always adopted in cavalry regiments. A bran-mash may be either made cold or hot. The latter is best made thus: Put the required quantity of bran into a stable-rubber and tie it up, and then let it steep for a short time in a bucket filled with enough boiling water to be absorbed by the bran. Wring the water out of the mash by twisting the neck of the rubber. Open the rubber and spread it out, so as to allow the mash to cool a little before giving.

A bran poultice may be made in the same way. I have described how to cook linseed as a mash. Bran-mash may be, if desired, mixed up with the linseed-mash.

Linseed-meal is used for poultices, and requires to be mixed with hot water. To make it properly, the *boiling* water should be poured into a vessel, as much of it as may be considered requisite for the purpose, and the linseed-meal gradually added to the water, and stirred round and round the same way until the poultice is of the required consistency.

Many horses will eat a linseed-mash and will not

touch gruel, and *vice versâ*, while others will take either.

Gruel is a capital thing to give to a tired horse, especially after hunting or on the way home. The reader should know how to make it for himself. Take a good double handful or more of oatmeal, and, having put it into a bucket, pour some *boiling* water over it and stir it round till it is like a thick cream; add a little more boiling water to it, and then pour in sufficient cold water to reduce it to a blood-heat, when a horse will drink it; and if he is *very* exhausted a wineglassful of gin or a bottle of warm ale may be added, but not *many* horses will take these stimulants.

When oatmeal is not procurable, *flour* may be substituted, and if *neither* is to be got, a bottle of beer may be poured down the throat by inserting the mouth of the bottle (the latter being wrapped round with a rubber) in the space between the tusk and grinders. I have often done this on cold or wet nights when camped out, and after a time my horses got to like it, and I am sure it did them good.

That 'a merciful man is merciful to his beast' is a saying well known enough, and surely the comfort of the animal which has so well and generously worked all day for you is worth a thought. Ay, and if you are an English gentleman and an

English sportsman, it will be your *first* thought, even before your *own* comfort. You will be well repaid in feeling that you have done the best you can for the dumb animal which is *yours* and dependent on your care. He will himself repay you also *for* that care, in that he will be none the less able to carry you well the next time—nay, perhaps all the better for it; and you will not lose the respect of your servants thereby, believe me.

CHAPTER XVIII.

Personal supervision by master.—Such personal supervision not lowering.—Evidences of a good groom.—Amount of work for one servant.—Overworked grooms.—Good servants procurable.—A fair day's work and a fair day's wage.—Hours for grooming.—Time required to clean a horse.—Blind horses, and summer coats.—'Wolf-teeth' and shying.—Hour for 'morning' stables.—Hours for, and routine of, grooming.—Morning.—Mid-day.—Evening.—Grooming a tired hunter. — Extra rules for grooming hunters.—Refusing corn.—Points to be specially attended to in grooming.—How to test good grooming.—How to groom.—The use of the curry-comb.—Clipping.—Time for clipping.—Singeing.—Naphtha and gas singeing-lamps.—Unclipped legs.—Treatment after singeing.—Mane-pulling.—How to pull a mane.—Hogging manes.—Tail-cutting.—Docking.

IF the eye of the master is to be over the servant, it is certainly essential that he should not only know what the work of that servant consists of, but also *how* it should be performed. Neither will it in any way detract from the master's dignity, or lessen his servant's respect for him, if the latter is aware that his master can himself show him with his own hands how his work should be done.

Many a time have I myself, being in uniform, taken the brush out of the hand of a recruit and shown him how to use it to the best advantage to his horse, and with the least necessary expenditure of force. I have more than once seen generals of cavalry, with their own hands, saddle and bridle a horse in order to better explain the meaning of some system which they were anxious to adopt, or to try, and on one occasion I distinctly remember seeing General Sir F. Fitzwygram seated on the top of a troop horse and busily employed in hauling away at baggage and wallet-straps, so as to explain to an officer how he wished these articles put on. I think after these remarks I need say no more. Such work is elevating, but I am well aware that there are plenty of men to be found, not the *gentlemen* of England though, who would think it utterly beneath them to do any such thing.

Rest assured that a little occasional supervision by the master, during the grooming-hour, will do no harm to those who know how grooming *ought* to be done. It is very apparent whether a groom knows and does his work properly, or is ignorant, or slurs it. The result of his labour will show if the latter is the case, and the very way he handles his grooming utensils the former; and when engaging a groom I like to see him at work myself for a few minutes if I can so arrange it. The way he sets about it will at once show me whether he is a groom or an impostor. I think that it will be an advantage to some of my readers if I endeavour to explain how a horse should be groomed.

First of all I must inform him that in a single-handed stable two horses are, if he has to exercise them or go out with a carriage, quite as much as a man can manage properly. Where a great many horses are kept one man to every three will suffice, or *should* do so. Two men can do a stable of five horses, provided that they are not both of them taken out with carriages, etc. To exercise and groom two horses and clean a carriage, and do the work *well*, is a hard day's work for any man, and he should never be taken away for other purposes. Of course, there are heaps of cases where a single man has to do a great deal more than this, but then the work is not, and *cannot*, be done as it should. The horses are not properly groomed; the carriage and harness are not kept up to the mark, and the man, being pressed for time, is never clean or well dressed, and instead of being able to turn out with his breeches and boots well cleaned and put on, they are very much the reverse, and probably he is compelled from press of work to cover his trousered legs and ill-cleaned boots with an apron or rug. Such a state of affairs is to me so very unlovely, that I would far sooner keep but one pony and turn it out *well*, than three horses, and have to put up with dirt and slovenliness. Let a man have a fair day's work to do, by all means, but let him have a fair day to do it in. If matters are thus arranged, insist upon every little detail being kept up to the highest possible pitch. Excuse *nothing*; allow of *no* excuse, unless it be through ignorance, and a groom is supposed to *know* his work. A good servant costs no more than a bad. People are for ever bemoaning the scarcity of good servants. It's all rubbish. There are *heaps* to be got—plenty of good, honest men, who both know their work and do it; but *every* man is not like this, and it is necessary to exercise due precaution, and perhaps to take some little trouble in the matter. People get bad servants very often because they won't take the trouble to get *good* ones.

'A fair day's work and a fair day's wage.' Let the master be just and considerate, and, above all, courteous to his servants, and let him in return exact *to the full* the duty they should give to him, insisting upon a willing and ready compliance with his orders; failing this, dismissal. If a difficulty is experienced in obtaining a good servant, it is, believe me, a far better plan to train a man who is steady, respectable, and anxious to learn. He will do far *less* harm than a bad servant who knows his work and does not do it, for every day he will be gaining knowledge and experience; and if the master is *able* to train him, or to overlook his work, he will know that no neglect of duty is likely to pass unnoticed.

A horse should be groomed three times daily, viz. : In the morning, at mid-day, and in the evening. The following stable hours are as good as any, viz.:

6 a.m. to 7 a.m.
11 a.m. to 1 p.m.
5.30 p.m. to 6.30 p.m.

No matter how dirty a horse may be, if he is in good condition, and his coat is not very heavy, an hour at most should be sufficient time for his being thoroughly dried and cleaned.

Of course, where horses have long winter coats on, and come in sweating profusely, they will very often 'break out,' as it is called, after they have been dried, and so have to be dried again ; but this is a special, and not an ordinary case, inasmuch as most horses are, with a view to prevent this, clipped during the winter, when their coats are long. It may, perhaps, interest the reader to know that horses which are blind do not get a proper summer coat, and I am informed, and indeed can quote cases in proof of the statement, that this is also equally so with horses who are blind in one eye only. No one seems, as yet, to have been able to assign any satisfactory reason for this being the case. If I may be permitted to hark back to a previous chapter, I should like to mention another almost equally curious fact, and one of which I was not aware till a few years ago. I have never experienced a case in my own stable, but I have been so assured by so many people that it most undoubtedly is true, that I am bound to believe it, inasmuch as my informants were all practical, and, I may further add, essentially truthful. It is this. Some horses have what are called 'wolf-teeth.' These teeth are situated just in front of the first grinders. It is by no means uncommon to find them in horses, but it is asserted that these teeth are very often the cause of a horse shying, and that they very much affect the sight at times. On their removal the habit of shying ceases. With an *ordinary* tooth I can quite understand that this may be the case, but since these 'wolf-teeth' have no fang, and are merely rudimentary, I am quite at a loss to tell how the sight can be affected by their presence. I have known cases in which horses have suffered from these teeth to an extent which has left no doubt in my mind that their sight is undoubtedly impaired by the irritation caused by them, and their eyes have become cloudy and dull. But as soon as the 'wolf-teeth' have been removed (and it is a very simple operation) the eyes have regained their natural colour and lustre. These facts, therefore, speak for themselves, but they somewhat puzzle me. But I must return to my subject, from which I have very much strayed. The following scale of work for a groom will be found useful. I have given 6 a.m. for the hour at which the day's duties should commence. Some people make their hours 5.30 in summer and 6.30 in winter. I consider that the same hour throughout the year is a better rule, and it is better to keep one regular hour, and insist on that hour being adhered to, than to change it.

6 A.M.: Water and feed with hay; rearrange any clothing which may have got wrong; pick out feet; sponge nostrils and dock; remove dung and the soiled part of the litter, and place bedding in the air (or, if raining, in the bedding-sheds) to dry; sweep out stall; remove clothing and bandages, and place them in the air; thoroughly clean body, legs, head, mane, and tail; clean headstall and replace it; put on fresh *day* clothing.

6.45 A.M.: Feed with corn; tidy up stable; arrange ventilators.

7 A.M.: Go to breakfast.

8 A.M. : Saddle and bridle for exercise; remove horse to spare stall (where possible) and thoroughly wash down stable and scrub out manger, once or twice a week, using a little salt for the latter

8.30 A.M. : Open all doors and windows (where such can be left open with safety), and go to exercise, which should be almost entirely walking, except in very cold weather, when a hood should be worn.

10 A.M.: Close windows (unless in warm weather); remove bridle, and put on headstall, and rack up horse; clean watering bridle, stirrup-leathers, irons.

11.15 A.M.: Remove saddle-clothing, bandages, etc., and thoroughly groom as before, finishing up with a damp (not over-wet) wisp and dry rubber; replace clothing, and (if necessary) handrub legs, and put on fresh bandages; litter down with fresh clean straw.

12 MID-DAY: Water, and feed with hay, and arrange stable thoroughly; clean saddle, brush and clean night clothing and bandages, and fold them up; turn and fork over-night bedding to assist its drying; clean up harness-room and rub over saddles, bridles, etc.

12.45 P.M. : Feed with corn.

1 P.M. : Go to dinner.

5.30 P.M. : Water and feed with hay; remove

dung, etc., and change clothing, etc., and give a third good grooming; replace day-clothing and bandages by night ditto; bring in night-bedding, and make up with that used during the day; brush out and clean stable.

6.15 P.M.: Feed with corn, and give remainder of hay; tidy up stable, etc.; lock up.

9.30 OR 10 P.M.: Visit stable again, removing dung, picking out feet, replacing hay which may have fallen; offer water again; see that everything is correct; arrange ventilators; lock up stable.

In the foregoing I have assumed that the horse has not been out hunting, or done any real work, during the day. Since a tired hunter is a good example to take for the purpose, we will suppose that such is the case, and that he has just come in, say, at the ordinary stable hour, 5.30 p.m. The following should be the routine of grooming observed: Remove bit, and put on headstall; slacken girths and remove stirrup-leathers; take off breast-plate; give a bucket of gruel or chilled water and hay; rub and dry ears; brush dirt off legs and feet; put on bandages loosely; dry neck, head, shoulders; sponge dock and nostrils; throw a rug over the horse and feed with linseed-mash or some corn. When this is finished, groom as much of the body as can be managed *without removing the saddle, which should be left on till the last thing.* Then remove saddle (this should never be taken off until at least half an hour has elapsed), thoroughly dry back, belly, and loins; give a good brisk grooming with a dry wisp, to assist in restoring the circulation; put on night-clothing; remove bandages, and finish drying and cleaning the legs; handrub them well; put on fresh bandages, and feed with corn again, and also hay; fork up and finish bedding; unrack so that the horse may roll if he will.

All this grooming should be done as quickly as it can be, and as thoroughly; for remember that your horse has had a hard day, and is longing to roll and rest. The stall should be ready for him on his return, and the bed made up, or nearly so. His mash, or whatever you may give him, should be ready for him *directly* he comes in, and his clothing and bandages should be warm and dry.

It will be observed that I have not said anything about washing either the legs or body. Such practices should never be permitted on such occasions, no matter how elaborate a system of douches, etc., may be provided in a stable. My reasons for this I will give later on, and they will, I think, be found sufficient. Any injury which a horse may have sustained after a day's hunting, etc., should be *at once* reported by the groom and be at once attended to, and all thorns, etc., should be carefully looked for and removed. The morning after a day's hunting the horse should be carefully examined and led out for a few minutes to see if he is sound. Later on in the day he may be led about for half an hour in as sheltered a spot as can be obtained.

If a horse refuses his corn at any time, the cause should be ascertained and proper treatment resorted to. Horses (other than excitable ones) do not refuse their corn except for some good reason. The sooner, therefore, that reason is known, the better for both horse and owner.

The above system of treatment for a tired hunter will serve equally well in the case of an ordinary horse, whether saddle or harness, under similar conditions.

In grooming a horse the following points should be particularly attended to : The ears, throat, inside the forearm, hocks, thighs, and heels should receive special care. It is in these places that it is perhaps more difficult to dry a horse and clean him, and it is there that a master will do well to examine his groom's work. If *these* are clean, the chances are that the rest of the horse is clean.

The throat is a place which is very often neglected and allowed to dry itself, hence, perhaps, the reason why so many horses become roarers.

Manes and tails, again, often do not receive the attention they should. Such take time and patience, especially where the hair is thick. A horse's mane and tail require to be carefully parted and well brushed at each parting.

If a horse is clean, no scurf or grease of any kind should ever adhere to the hand when rubbed over the skin. If your groom assures you to the contrary, and says that you must expect a *little*, he lies, and knows it too. Perhaps in the spring and autumn, when coats are rising and falling, such an excuse may be *more* permissible, but even *then*, if a groom works hard, he can prevent grease and scurf being present.

In grooming, a groom should stand somewhat *away* from his horse, and by means of a straight arm he will gain additional power from the weight of his body. When a horse is sweating, much hard grooming and rubbing will not dry him as quickly as light, brisk wisping with straw. Until a horse is quite *dry* he cannot be cleaned.

The scurf collected in the body-brush should be removed by the curry-comb, and the latter from time to time cleared out by being tapped on the *floor* of the stable, and *not* into the manger or against the stall partitions.

In the cavalry the men are taught to tap out their curry-combs at the edge of the stall-posts. Their work is then apparent, as, if they have been doing their duty, there will be a heap of scurf to prove it.

Since it is necessary to remove a horse's coat during the winter, it is as well to consider how this is to be best done.

In the old days horses were clipped with a pair of scissors, or else shaved. Both of these operations were necessarily somewhat laborious, and the latter dangerous as well. Of late years the clipping machine has rendered these old-fashioned practices obsolete. The machine answers the purpose for which it is intended admirably, and the man who can cut a horse with it must indeed be a clumsy hand. Of course, as may be supposed, it leaves the marks of its teeth, however skilfully it may be used, and, moreover, does not take off the hair quite as closely as is desirable, so it is necessary when a horse has been clipped to level the coat still further by singeing it.

No horse's coat should ever be clipped until it is set. This is known by the appearance of long hairs, known as 'cat-hairs,' and when these show the coat may fairly be assumed to be ready for clipping. If a horse is clipped too soon, he will never have the same appearance as if the proper time is waited for, and it will be a source of trouble all the winter through.

It is a custom in some stables, and a good one too, never to *clip* horses, but to begin singeing them down early in the autumn directly they begin to show any signs of thickening, and to keep on doing this constantly through the winter. By such means, though perhaps more troublesome, a horse's coat is kept in as perfect a state as it can well be under the circumstances, and I am convinced that it is the best way of keeping a winter coat down.

As I have remarked in a former chapter, there are two kinds of singeing-lamps—that for use with gas and that for naphtha—and I there stated my reasons for preferring the use of the latter, as it is less likely to burn a horse, and burns the hair more steadily and thoroughly than the fiercer flame of the gas; but whichever description of lamp may be used, either of them requires to be constantly attended to and cleared. The naphtha is more troublesome in this respect than the gas, and the wick requires to be shifted now and again. It is, moreover, necessary that when a groom is singeing he should keep a damp rag in his left hand, ever ready to quench the coat should it catch fire, as also to avoid singeing too close to the roots of the mane and tail.

For saddle horses, the part of the back where the saddle goes should never be clipped or singed, but the saddle having been carefully fitted on the back, the hair should be neatly clipped round in its shape.

It has of late years been very much the custom to leave the legs of horses unclipped. It was a fashion which was brought over from Ireland, and was supposed to be a protection to the legs, and to prevent thorns and stone walls, etc., damaging them. I never did agree with it, simply because I thought it looked horrid, and because I do not consider that it *is* a protection. If all the hair off a horse's legs were to be collected together, the whole of it could be held in one hand, and I do not see that *it is* any advantage, and am quite sure that many a blow, and many a thorn which would be seen at once were the legs clipped, is often left undiscovered until lameness or the existence of matter makes the injury apparent. Some people assert that it is a protection against mud-fever. I will, however, endeavour in another place to show that mud-fever can be very easily prevented by other means. Anyhow, I am glad to say the fashion has gone out, and in the shires unclipped legs are rarely to be seen.

After a horse is clipped and singed he requires to be thoroughly well groomed, and then galloped in clothing till he sweats well; after which he may be washed quickly with warm water, and should be thoroughly dried, and clothed up and bandaged until he has got perfectly cool and there is no danger of his suffering from chill, when he should be *again* groomed and well wisped, and his ordinary clothing replaced. If a horse is clipped at the right time, he should not require more than one, or at most two subsequent clippings during the season. His coat must then be left to grow for the spring, and must not be again touched, or his summer coat will be spoiled.

It is by no means an easy matter to pull a mane properly, but it is necessary, where the growth of hair is thick and long, to get rid of a good deal of it. There is a sort of infernal machine, called a mane-drag, a thing like a bent fork, which is used to drag the hair out of a mane. It is very aptly named. Drag it it does, and to a cruel extent, and inasmuch as it takes up a good lot at a time, it must be an unpleasant sensation to a horse. Dealers use them a good deal. I have noticed that some horses will not stand their manes being pulled ever so gently. The remembrance of the mane-drag has probably not faded from their minds. Of course, to *cut* a mane is but a tom-fool's work (I do not refer to what is called hogging a mane). If a mane is cut, as may be supposed, the hairs, when growing again, stand up through the longer hairs like a sort of chevaux-de-frise, and are hardly ornamental, if peculiar. Only dealers' grooms seem to thoroughly understand the art of pulling a mane properly. True that they do it in a rough, cruel fashion, as I have remarked, but that is rather because they have to smarten up a horse all at once for sale, and are pressed for time. A mane should not be pulled from the *underneath* side; and most certainly not from the *upper*. Therefore it must be pulled from the *middle*. In order to do this properly, the mane should be parted evenly, and the longer hairs, not more than two or three at a time, being held in the fingers of one hand, the remaining hairs should be run back clear of them, and a sharp, quick twitch being given, they are removed. It is impossible without cruelty to remove very much at a time; a little each day will soon thin a mane properly, and if thus carried out the hair will fall in light, thin locks, and give an appearance of style and breeding, which a thick, long, heavy mane cannot. A mane should never be pulled so that its edge is in a straight line. Clumsy grooms are very apt to do this, as it is easier and less tedious than to pull it as I have described.

For ponies, and anything *under* 14 hands, I consider hogging a mane is decidedly an *improvement*. Anything *over* that height should *never* be hogged. When a mane is hogged, the hair should be cut *quite* close down, and finished in a low, level ridge, but cut as short as it *can* be. A mane hogged after the fashion of the Parthenon horses is *not* smart. It is the fashion, in all but racehorses, to cut horses' tails short, and it has a smart appearance, and improves the appearance of a horse considerably; but it is a difficult matter to cut a tail well, and it must be remembered that it must be cut so that when the horse is going, and carrying it out, the cut edge is parallel to the ground. Nothing looks worse than to see the stump of the tail, when the latter has been docked, sticking up in the air end on, as it were. When a horse's tail is handled, he generally tries to tuck it in, and so the right angle for cutting must be judged when it is carried naturally. Docking horses after they are a certain age is cruel. It is, I fear, cruel at *any* time, and should never be done except by a skilful veterinary surgeon. It should be done as quickly and carefully as possible. It requires a cool operator to do it well. I have known the most distressing scenes occur when docking has been attempted by a nervous bungler.

CHAPTER XIX.

Shoeing.—Odd feet indicative of previous unsoundness.—Construction of foot.—Shape and structure of crust and sole.—The frog.—Thickness of crust and sole.—Alæ of coffin-bone.—Circular action of foot.—Use of shoes.—Iron suitable for shoes.—Sole not to be pared.—Ignorance of farriers.—Evils of chopping out the heels.—Lowering the feet.—Shoe to rest on the crust.—Shape and thickness of shoe.—Clinches.--Position of nails.—Concave shoes.—'Fitzwygram' shoes.—The 'Charlier' system.—Tips.—Roughing.—Patent hoof-pads.—Calkins.—Over-reaching.—Cause of cutting and prevention.—Bevelled shoes.—Inconvenience caused by neglect of servants.—Inspection by farrier.—Shoeing-pricks.—Price of shoeing.—Hot feet and remedy.—Stopping.—Recipe for stopping.—Thrush and treatment.—Corns and treatment.—Shoeing with leather.—Lameness.—Shoulder lameness.—Lameness in hock; from splint; of fetlock-joint.—Sandcrack and treatment.—Hoof-ointment.

WE now have to consider *one* of the most important, if not *the* most important, subjects with which we have to deal in the present work, viz.: that of shoeing.

No matter how good in every other respect a horse may be, if his feet are not good and sound he is useless. We cannot utilize him, Pegasus-like, and make him fly. His feet have to sustain *him*, and any additional weight he may have to carry. If, therefore, he cannot carry *himself*, it is hardly to be expected that he can carry anything else.

One of the first lessons I ever received in the selection of horses was given me by one of the best judges I have ever known. His advice to me was as follows, viz. : Let your inspection begin at the feet. If they are not good, and are not exactly the same shape and size (the forefeet, of course), have nothing whatever to do with the horse. Make any excuse you like, but make up your mind *not* to buy him, and, if you can, turn resolutely away from him. No advice *could* have been better. It was a beginning at the right end—the beginning itself. The feet of a horse are naturally *exactly* alike, and *invariably* so. If there is the *slightest* difference in their shape, it may be at once assumed, no matter how much you may be assured to the contrary, that that horse has been lame either in the foot, leg, or shoulder at some time or other, and probably lame for some long time. According as the difference is little or great, and from disuse, the structure of the foot has become more or less altered. Now, before entering any further upon the subject of shoeing, it will be well for us to briefly consider what a horse's foot really is like.

As may be seen on examining any well-preserved specimen, it consists of bones and horn. There are three bones, viz. : (1) The foot, pedal, or coffin bone, as it is termed. This is the principal bone, and is made to fit the horn covering (as seen in the specimen). (2) The navicular bone, which is at the back of the coffin-bone—this latter a small bone of peculiar shape. (3) The shorter pastern-bone, which is made to articulate on the top of the coffin-bone. This bone is, again, met by the *longer* pastern-bone, but as this latter is somewhat *above* the foot, we will omit further reference to it here.

Now, all these bones fit into each other, and are bound and knit together by ligaments, etc. If the horny portion of the foot is now examined, it will be seen to consist of two parts, viz. : the crust or wall, and the sole.

In the perfect foot the crust is nearly round. The *inner* side is slightly less so than the outer.

The top of the crust is smaller in diameter than the bottom ; a line drawn from the top (which is where the hair and hoof meet, and which is called the 'coronet') to the toe would form, in a perfect foot, an angle of 45° with the sole.

If the crust and sole are placed under a magnifying glass, it will be seen that, whereas the horn of both consists of a number of fine tubes which are filled with a moist oily substance—which is really the lubricating oil, and supplied for the purpose of keeping the horn tough and moist—the fibres of the crust run in a vertical direction, whilst those of the sole run laterally, and are interwoven with the fibres of the crust.

If the foot be now placed with the toe downwards, the sole being towards the observer, a sharp V-shaped growth will be noticed, which extends from the heel to about two-thirds of the distance between the heel and the toe. It is, as I have said, shaped like a V, but like a V whose ends have been looped round. This is what is called the 'frog,' and its looped ends are termed the 'bars.' These latter, doubling back as I have endeavoured to describe, meet the crust some little distance from the heels.

The use of the frog is to prevent a horse from slipping; and it is admirably adapted for the purpose, needless to remark, as is anything in Nature. The provisions made by Nature fail only when man's ignorance mars her handiwork. Now examine the inside of the foot, and it will be seen that the fibres are very apparent, and present the appearance of a species of coral, which I know well enough by sight, but I do not know its correct name. It is composed of a number of fan-like blades, radiating from the centre—laminated, in fact. The inside of the foot of a horse is thus laminated; and these are called the 'sensitive laminæ,' in contradistinction to the outer portion, which is formed of 'insensitive laminæ'—answering to the quick in the human nail and the growth from it.

I trust I may have been able to make my meaning clear enough; but it is a somewhat difficult matter to be explicit on such a subject without the aid of either specimen or illustration. A more gifted writer than I am could, doubtless, make a better business of it, but then he might perhaps use long words, and I wish to avoid their use as much as possible, so that even a groom can understand what I may treat of herein.

We have examined the foot of a horse inside and out, and its shape to a certain extent. If it is still further inspected, it may be observed that while the thickness of the sole, except where the frog is situated, is pretty much the same throughout, that of the crust varies very considerably, and that it is very much thicker at the toe than at the heel, and gradually becomes thinner (narrower) as it approaches the heel; that the *inner* side of the foot is also slightly thinner than the outside, and that where it is thick at the sole it is very thin at the coronet.

It will be well perhaps to again take up the coffin-bone, and it will be noticed that at its ends (the heel ends) it branches out into two thin, wing-shaped formations. These are, indeed, termed the alæ, or wings. Attached to these wings are two gristly formations. As I have to say something regarding these later on, I think the present a good opportunity for drawing attention to them, as it is the ossification of these which causes what are termed 'side-bones.'

I will now ask the reader to take note of the action of a horse, at any pace he may select, and to observe the way the foot is brought down to, and removed from, the ground, and he will see that, though the foot comes *flat* down, the action of the leg is circular, and he will easily follow me when I endeavour to explain to him that, by this circular motion of the leg, the toe of a horse's foot would become very much worn, more so than any other part. Such is the case; and if a worn-out shoe is examined, it will be seen that the iron, while worn nearly through at the toe, is but little the worse for wear at the heel or elsewhere.

I think I have now made mention of all that is necessary for me to impress on the reader with regard to the structure of the foot, and I trust I have not been over-verbose; but it has been necessary to study the conformation of the foot before we can determine what sort of shoe will fit it.

Were horses required to work on soft ground only, they would not require any shoes at all. Indeed, there *are* some horses whose feet are so hard and flinty, and the horn of such wonderful texture, and its growth so rapid, that they can work on *any* ground unshod; but these cases are few and far between, and though several people have written on the subject of using horses *without* shoes, and have tried to abandon their use, it has never been adopted generally; and except here and there, as a sort of craze, it is not likely to obtain favour, since there are so few horses which can stand the wear and tear of our roads without shoes.

Now let us inquire what the use of a shoe is.

The answer, of course, is this, viz. : To protect a horse's foot from breaking or sustaining too much wear, thereby becoming sore, when ridden or driven on hard ground, such as our macadamized roads of the present day, etc.

Nothing further than this is required; yet it is most difficult to effect this in a simple and sensible manner. One thing is certain, and that is, that there is no substance which we know of, as yet discovered, which will answer the purpose as well as iron. The edge of the crust is what it is necessary to protect; nothing further. How best to do this is another question.

We have agreed that the protection given must be an iron one, and that it must be of a certain thickness, in order that it may wear a reasonable time.

There are some dozens of different patterns of shoes—scores, I may say. I myself have ever so many; and of all the people who have invented them, *but one* only seems to me to have arrived at what a shoe should be, and that pattern is what is called the 'Charlier,' named after its inventor. But as this shoe necessitates a system entirely its own, and the latter requires a careful and skilled workman to carry out, it is not in as general use as it should be. The foot requires careful preparation, and tools specially made for such. Moreover, we English people are dreadful bigots, and are very slow to adopt a new system. I myself have tried all sorts, kinds, and descriptions of shoes on my horses—the 'Charlier' amongst them—and I can therefore speak from experience; and I say most truthfully when I declare this to be not only by far the best *I* know of, but to be the *one* and *only* shoe which has ever yet been invented fit to use; and I have not a single word of anything but praise to say for it. I do not know M. Charlier, nor have

I ever seen him; so I have no interest in the success of his shoe financially. I only praise it because it is worthy of all praise; and were I able to find a farrier within reach of my home to whom I could entrust the shoeing of my horses by the 'Charlier' system, I should most certainly not use any other kind of shoe in my stable.

After this eulogy, the reader will probably wish to know what manner of shoe the 'Charlier' shoe is. Before I proceed to explain, it is necessary for me to state that, inasmuch as Nature did *not* intend a horse to travel on macadamized roads, so she equally *did* intend that the sole of a horse's foot should come in contact with the ground; and if such is prevented, the sole, from disuse, must necessarily become shrunken and lose vitality, as would any one of our own members become weak and feeble if we were to forbear using it. Thus, if we were to always carry one arm in a sling, and never use it, it would waste. Therefore, for the sole of a horse's foot to be kept in a healthy state, and for the horn to grow well and strong, it must be *used*.

Again, if it were necessary for a person to walk over a rough or hard road for several miles, he would hardly be likely to elect to do so in pumps; rather would he don his thickest shooting-boots—

and why? Of course, to protect his feet from being bruised by stones, etc. Nature has provided that the sole of a horse's foot should be thick, and sufficiently so to protect the foot from possible bruises, nor could any substance have been better devised for the purpose than horn. Yet the *wilful pigheadedness*, the *crass* ignorance, of farriers, persists in cutting away the very protection which Nature has given the horse, and paring and hollowing out the sole. You may ask why. *I* can't tell you; nor can they. 'It has been the custom,' they say; they can give no other reason. They pare away the sole; they cut away the crust; they rasp the delicate fibres so as to *encourage* the horn, so exquisitely designed by Nature to be tough, to become brittle; every stroke of the hateful rasp tears open and destroys numberless conduits of lubricating oil—and why? again I may repeat. Simply and solely because, it being their *trade* to fit a shoe to a horse's foot, they, being too clumsy to do so, fit the horse's foot to the shoe. Horn is such a pleasant, easy material to cut and carve at, and looks so nice when smeared over with some filthy black oil—and iron is *so hard*; it takes such a lot of labour, and it is so very difficult to make the shoe fit as it should. That is the *reason*, and if they were honest, that is what they would answer.

Such men are not *workmen*; they are bunglers: they are not farriers; they should have been carpenters.

It makes me feel hot and angry as I write this, and feel inclined to dig my pen into the very paper, wishing all the time that the paper were but one of such so-called farriers.

Another malpractice is also common amongst farriers. They chop out the heel, so that when a horse's foot is viewed from behind, after they have been at work, it has the appearance of a very neatly carved W. Of course that is *also* the custom. Therein they speak the truth, sadly truthfully. Now, since a circle is the *perfection* of form, and perfection of form is perfection of strength, it well accords with the rest of the work to destroy that form. Take for example a wooden ring. So long as it is intact, it is strong; cut half an inch out of it, and its strength is gone: it bends in and breaks. This is precisely the effect which chopping out the heel has upon the horse's foot. It bends in.

Horn will grow, it is true; we wish it to do so. Its growth is the very life and soul of a sound, good foot.

If, however, a horse's foot is prevented from wearing by means of a shoe, it is obvious that in time it will grow too long, and it must therefore be shortened. This growth requires removing once a month, as a general rule, and, as a general rule also, shoes require renewing, under ordinary conditions, once a month. Therefore it is not requisite that a shoe should be any thicker than is necessary to last that time.

As the sole of the foot is, for the purpose of strength, constructed so as to be somewhat concave, it does not require to be cut down, and should never be touched further than to trim off any ragged growths from the frog. All superfluous horn will flake out, and in a healthy foot will preserve its concavity sufficiently to obviate any necessity for its being lowered.

The crust, on the contrary, *must* be lowered, and the month's growth removed; but no *more* than this amount should be taken off; and in this lowering care must be taken that both feet are left of exactly the same length, and that each foot is *perfectly level* and *true to the ground*. That is all that should be done; nothing more is required; anything further than that is not only unnecessary, but harmful. The foot is now ready for the shoe to be fitted on. I have shown that the crust is thicker at the toe than at the heel. The crust is the portion of the foot on which the shoe must rest— on it, and it *alone*, and *not* on the sole. The shoe, therefore, must so fit the foot that it bears only on the crust, and it should therefore, in order to do this, follow in its shape that of the crust, and inasmuch as the greatest amount of wear is at the toe, that portion of the shoe should be thicker than elsewhere, so as to withstand the wear and tear. Inversely, as but little wear takes place at the heel, there is no need for the iron to be as thick there as at the toe.

It will be seen, therefore, that the shoe should be both narrower and thinner as it approaches the heel. Thick, wide metal becomes useless lumber. A shoe, also, should not project beyond the edges of the crust, especially on the inside, as the latter would very probably interfere with the action, and the horse be badly cut and damaged; and if it projects on the outer side, it is not only useless, but likely to pull off in deep ground.

A shoe should be plenty *long* enough at the heels, but not too long. If too short, it will sink into the heel and cause corns and other evils; if too long, it will pull off, and also be in the way.

The only plan I know of which really answers, by which to fasten the shoe to the foot, is by nailing it on, through holes in the shoe, obliquely through the crust. The ends of the projecting nails are then turned down ('clinched,' as it is termed), any superfluous length being broken off. These clinches are made with a hammer. Their ends may be rasped slightly, but in doing this care must be exercised to prevent the rasp touching the crust.

The toe and fore-quarters of the crust being the thicker—*i.e.*, the *wider*—parts, they are the best suited for the purpose of nailing the shoe on to. *Four*, or at most *five*, nails are sufficient to fasten a shoe. If five are used, *three* will be on one side and two on the other; and since the outer side of the crust is somewhat thicker than the inner, the three should be placed on the outside. The two inner nails should not be opposite to the outer ones, but divide the two spaces between the three.

The heads of the nails should not project above the nail-holes, since it is evident that if they *do* so they wear first of all, and the shoe must drop off. They should therefore be countersunk, and fit the nail-holes exactly—the punch which is used for making the nail-holes corresponding exactly with the size and shape of the heads of the nails.

Now, it is very possible that if a shoe is perfectly flat on the side next to the ground, a stone may lodge between it and the frog, and possibly cause a horse to fall or bruise the foot. It is therefore advisable that it should be made concave on its inner edge, from where the line of the crust would come—hollowed out, as it were—and rounded so as to prevent the possibility of a stone lodging against it.

A horse invariably travels (if his feet are not overgrown) better on old shoes than on new, inasmuch as, the toe being worn by the circular motion of the foot which I have above referred to, he is saved the extra exertion of having to raise his foot somewhat higher than necessary in order to clear the ground.

General Sir F. Fitzwygram—of whom I have before made mention, and who has done very much towards improving the shoeing of horses, and has written more common-sense on the subject than anyone else—invented a form of shoe which was made at the toe after the fashion of a worn shoe, only that the toe was made thick enough to stand the month's wear. The toe being turned up, necessitates the crust being slightly cut away at the toe to receive it.

Next to the 'Charlier,' this pattern of shoe is the very best ever produced, and it has been with this pattern and his system in my mind that I have written the above; indeed, the shoe I have just described is, as near as I can make it, what is termed a 'Fitzwygram' shoe.

I will now proceed to explain the 'Charlier' system, which I can the more easily do after the foregoing.

The preparation of the foot for shoeing on the 'Charlier' system is as follows: The *crust* of the foot is lowered to the extent of about one-third of an inch the whole way round by means of a gauge. The shoe, which is made from a bar of soft iron, rectangular in shape, and of equal width and thickness (about one-third of an inch each way), is fitted into this groove or rebate which has been formed by the gauge, and which it exactly corresponds with. Thus the sole of the foot is brought on to the ground, and the edge of the crust is prevented from wearing by the shoe. By this system the foot is used as it should be, and yet sufficiently protected. The shoe is light, and wears well, and never comes off. Every part of the foot is kept healthy by its use. The frog is able to perform its work, and its growth is therefore vigorous, and it is less likely to suffer from thrush, etc. The very lightness, too, of the shoe tends to diminish the concussion which is caused by the use of a greater amount of metal.

The first time I made use of the 'Charlier' shoe I did so by the advice of a friend. I had at the time a very good-looking, well-bred mare, whose feet were somewhat contracted. I had bought her cheap, otherwise I should not have taken her into my stable. After she had been shod on the 'Charlier' system for some four months her feet had nearly recovered their normal size, having expanded to the extent of about one-sixteenth of an inch. Had I persevered with her, I doubtless could have brought them back to their proper size; but I sold her to a friend, and I regret to say she had to be shot very soon afterwards, her leg having been broken by a kick from another horse. This is only one of several instances which I could adduce to prove the advantage of the system.

I should not, however, advise that a horse should be *at once* put fully on to 'Charlier' shoes, but rather that they should be adopted gradually, the depth of the groove being made deeper at each successive shoeing, until the full depth is reached. My reason for saying this is that, as a rule, horses' feet have been so pared and tinkered about, and the sole, from disuse, become so weak and shrunken, that they are not in a fit condition to be *at once* put on to the ground and to do their proper work. In three months, however, they should be quite ready for it.

The legs and feet of a horse which is properly

shaped are straight, and consequently the action of the foot is true to the front. Some horses—indeed, many—whose conformation in this respect is defective, do not move their feet truly to the front. They may turn in; they may turn out—'winding' and 'dishing,' as it is termed. Again, horses which are what is called 'calf-kneed' throw their feet about in the most peculiar fashion, and are very apt to 'box' their ankles and to knock themselves about very much. If such horses were unshod, they could not hit themselves. In these cases the 'Charlier' system is very advantageous, but where an *ordinary* shoe is used, it often becomes a very difficult matter to prevent their hitting themselves.

It may be necessary to shoe the horse so that one side of the foot is lower than the other. Our friend the farrier suggests that the shoe should be made thicker or thinner on one side. For a *short* time this *may* answer, but as soon as the shoe gets worn (and such horses wear their shoes very irregularly), the evil again occurs. A 'three-quarter' shoe, as it is termed, is then tried. That answers, perhaps, until the end of the shoe (being only half its proper length on one side of the foot), sinking into the foot, probably causes lameness. Of course there *is* a right and a wrong way, and we have been supposing the wrong. The right way is not to alter the shoe, but to lower the foot more on one side than the other, and thus the required level is obtained. Such lowering must be, however, but slight and carefully done.

The use of tips is often recommended. They are nothing but very short shoes. A horse *cannot* work long on them on hard ground; the heels get worn and sore, as they wear sooner than the iron, and, as may be supposed, there is then undue strain placed on the tendons at the back of the leg. The ends of the tips, moreover, sink into the foot and cause corns, etc.

It is the custom in frosty weather to have the shoes roughed or turned up. This consists in the heels being turned so as to present the *ends* of the shoes to the ground, and so prevent slipping. Nothing else seems to quite answer the purpose, yet this system is far from being a satisfactory one, inasmuch as the shoes are thus too short, and the heels being unduly raised, the proper position of the foot is altered, and if used for any length of time corns and enlarged joints are the result.

There is a very good description of foot-pad made of indiarubber, and which is constructed so as to be readily fitted to the foot of a horse without removing the shoe, and it is as easily taken off when not required. A pair of pincers are made for the purpose of fitting the springs to which the indiarubber is attached, and sold with them. The pad is also split, to allow of the frog coming through. I have never used them, but from what I have been told by those who have, I believe them to be excellent, and to fulfil the purpose for which they are intended—viz., to prevent horses slipping in frosty weather, etc.—very thoroughly, and I should advise their adoption in preference to the system of turning up. They are sold in various sizes. I think their price is about half a guinea and upwards, for a set of four.

Calkins are lumps of metal which are welded on to the heels of the hind-shoes for harness work, to keep horses from slipping. Their use is chiefly confined to cart and heavy horses, and horses which work on roads which are heavily paved. They may be styled 'necessary evils.'

Horses—hunters especially—are very apt to cut themselves when galloping through deep ground, or in jumping. This is called overreaching, and is produced by bad shoeing. It is very commonly, and mistakenly, supposed that the injury is inflicted by the toe of the *hind*-shoe striking the heel or back of the foreleg. If such a cut is examined, it will be seen to be of a crescent shape, and not that which would be inflicted by the toe of the hind-shoe. The injury is really done by the *inside edge* of the toe of the hind-shoe. Where a hind-shoe is made flat, if its edge is felt it will be at once seen how sharp the latter is ; and it becomes more so the more the shoe is worn. It will be observed, too, that the shape of the cut exactly corresponds in shape with this edge. The edge, therefore, must be removed, and all hind-shoes should be made quite round on their inner edges, as round as it is possible to make them. If roughly done, they will soon wear to a sharp edge ; but if this is properly carried out, even *should* a horse hit himself, he will not cut. An overreach is a nasty and troublesome thing to cure, and I have seen horses whose heels have been completely cut off by reason of their hind-shoes having been improperly made. 'Clicking' or 'forging,' as it is termed, viz., the hind shoe striking against the edge of the fore, is also prevented by the use of bevelled shoes, such as I have described.

Grooms should be taught to be careful to examine the shoes of their horses, both *before* and *after* work, and to see that they are on firmly, and that they have not shifted, and also that the clinches have not risen. Anything which is wrong should be immediately rectified. Can anything be more provoking than to discover, just as a horse is wanted, that a visit to the farrier's shop is necessary, because the groom has been too careless to examine the shoes in proper time? It may be a matter of almost life and death to catch a train at a particular time, and the horse is useless. The station may be a long way off and the farrier's shop not within easy reach. Again, a day's hunting may be lost because of such carelessness. Such lost days are sure, too, to be 'good scenting days.' Where practicable, let me advise the reader, if a hunting man, to arrange with the farrier to always visit his stable at such an hour on a hunting morning, that, if anything *is* wrong, there may be time to have it put right before starting. If the *morning* visit cannot be arranged, let him come the day before; but the morning is the best time, as it is quite possible that a fidgety or nervous horse may, in kicking at night, as such horses are very apt to do, displace or break a shoe, and it is as well to be on the safe side.

A good and careful farrier should *never* prick a horse in shoeing, *i.e.*, should never drive a nail into the quick. I fear that but few horses escape this at some time or other during the year. Whenever a horse's foot is hot, and it has been recently shod, it may be generally assumed that it has been pricked. The shoe must be at once removed, and the suspected nail-hole searched and poulticed with a linseed-meal poultice. As a rule, the horse is sound again in a few days, if thus promptly treated. If you can persuade your farrier to do so, let him sign an agreement with you to pay a fine of five shillings for every time he pricks your horse, and in order to further induce care on his part, promise him a substantial Christmas-box if he does not prick any of your horses during the year.

The usual price paid for shoeing is 1s. per foot. In order to secure extra good work, it will be wise to offer 5s. a shoeing.

When horses have been working on very hard ground and in hot weather, their feet are apt at times to get hot from the concussion, and it is well to cool them with a wet swab made of felt, and which can be loosely buckled round the fetlock. Some horses are very subject to hot feet. It is evidence of weakness of constitution, and should be alleviated as much as possible.

If it is required at any time to soften the feet of a horse by reason of the horn having become brittle, which, by the way, it will not become in a healthy foot, the feet may be 'stopped,' as it is called. Clay and cow-dung mixed together are generally used for this purpose, and the latter is very cooling. Horse-dung is as heating to the foot as cow-dung is cooling; hence the necessity for never allowing dung to remain in a stable, and for keeping a horse's feet constantly cleared of it. Stopping may be well used the night before shoeing.

A very good and more cleanly stopping than the above is made by mixing Stockholm tar, soft soap, and linseed-meal together in equal quantities. It may be kept in a jar to be used as required.

Good feet well cared for do not require the use of any stopping.

Thrush is a diseased frog. It is caused by dirt and neglect, by a horse being allowed to stand in dung, and also by bad shoeing, the frog being not properly used. It is a disgrace to any stable. Its presence is generally patent to anyone who enters the stable. No need to ask if it is there; your nostrils inform you of the fact soon enough. The first thing to be done towards curing it is to thoroughly clean and wash the foot, and to remove any decayed edges; and to dress the parts affected with the following, which may be used by inserting pledgets of tow saturated with it between the clefts of the frog, viz.: one part carbolic acid, eight parts oil. This should be used daily. Bedding of beech-sawdust will help to hasten a cure. The horse should, as soon as possible, be shod so that his frogs bear on the ground. Tips will do for this purpose for a *time*. Any means which will ensure dryness and pressure on the frog will tend to effect a cure. If thrush is neglected worse evil in the form of canker may ensue.

Corns in a horse are caused by too short shoes; the heels not being sufficiently long, their ends pressing on the foot bruise it, and inflammation is soon set up. Corns are generally to be found in the *inner* side of the foot. What is called the 'seat of corn' is just at the point where the bars and crust meet. They cause considerable lameness, and may, if neglected, become *very* serious, and a sinus being established, the matter lodged forces its way upward and out through the coronet, and forms what is called a 'quittor,' which is a fistulous sore. The remedy for corns consists of the following treatment, viz.: Remove the shoe at once; have the corn pared out so far as it extends (this should be done by a competent person); poultice, if necessary, with a linseed or bran poultice; shoe with a tip until the foot has grown sufficiently to bear an ordinary shoe. It is better to abstain from working a horse suffering from bad corns until it is cured. Corns are most difficult and troublesome to cure, and they require *thorough* treatment to prevent any tendency to recur. It is a most inexcusable thing for a horse to suffer from corns, and is *entirely* due to bad shoeing. Some horses are more liable to them than others, especially horses with short, straight pasterns. It is at times advisable to shoe a horse with leather—that is to say, with leather between the foot and the shoe. The way this is done is thus: A piece of thick leather, large enough to cover the whole foot, is laid over the sole of the foot, and is then fastened on when the nails are driven. The outside superfluous leather is then trimmed off, and it is essential that the whole of the leather which covers the sole should also be removed. This method of shoeing is resorted to in order to lessen the concussion arising from hard roads, etc.

When a horse is lame, the first step towards curing him of his lameness is to discover *where* he is lame—on which leg; whether the lameness is above or below the knee, and if below, whether it is in the foot or leg. If a *man* is lame, anybody short of a fool can tell which is the lame leg, because when he walks he limps; in other words, he uses the lame leg less than the sound one. He stands, *dwells* on the sound one, and puts no more strain on the *lame* one than he is forced to do. This is precisely what a lame horse does. He dwells on the sound leg, and 'dots' on the lame one. Yet, simple as it may appear to be from the above to determine which leg a horse is lame upon, I can assure the reader that there are, comparatively speaking, but *very few* people who are able to tell. I have known even a veterinary surgeon mistaken — more than once, too — though, of course, it was inexcusable on his part to be unable to say with certainty at once. A man has but two legs, a horse has four. If the reader will take the trouble to first of all note the action of the forelegs, and carefully mark the cadence as each foot comes to the ground, he will, if the horse is lame in *front*, see at *once* that the foot of the lame leg (except in cases of shoulder lameness, when the toe is dragged along the ground) is a shorter time on the ground than the sound one. If the horse is not lame in front, he must be lame behind. To detect *which* leg is equally easy with the *hind* legs as with the *front*. Standing straight behind the horse, as he is trotted away from you, watch the hocks as they are brought up in succession, and the lame leg can at once be detected. In cases where the lameness is very slight and difficult to catch, it is a good plan to hold a stick horizontally in both hands, looking under its under edge, bringing the latter down to such a level that, as the hocks are brought up, they, as it were, touch it; any difference in action can then more readily be observed. The lame leg having been discovered, it is necessary to decide whether the lameness is above or below the knee or hock. This is not always an easy matter, unless there is anything very apparent to warrant a conclusion. If in the shoulder, it is generally accompanied by a dragging of the toe. If in the hock, the way the hock of the lame leg is flexed will generally indicate it. If the horse is lame from splint, he generally bobs his head as the lame foot touches the ground, and the splint can be felt. If in the fetlock joint, it will probably be swollen. If in the foot, there is (except in one instance—navicular disease) sure to be heat in the seat of lameness.

There are cases where a really experienced veterinary surgeon is very often puzzled to diagnose the exact ailment at once. But whenever the lameness is supposed to be in the foot, it is a good and safe plan to have the shoe at once removed carefully and gently, and if possible let the master stand by while the removal is being effected, in order to prevent the farrier knocking the foot about unnecessarily. In such a case the veterinary surgeon ought to be consulted, and the shoe having been already removed will save time. When sending for a veterinary surgeon it is always better to *write*, and to state in the letter, as nearly as possible, the circumstances of the case, instructing him, should no reliable farrier be within reach, to bring one with him; and see that anything he may require in the way of hot water, etc., is ready against his arrival.

It is curious that where horses have one or more of their feet white, the white is always more liable to disease than the darker-coloured ones. The horn of a white foot is never as tough and good as that of a dark foot, and yet a white or gray horse is generally a good one. I may here remark that if there are any two colours which bespeak hardiness and general goodness more than another, black-brown and gray are those colours. I think, for choice, the former, especially when accompanied, as it often is, with a tan muzzle.

But to return to what I was saying. If a horse is lame and he *has* a white leg or foot, the chances are that the lame leg or foot is the white one. Chestnut horses are very apt to go in the feet, more so than those of any other colour, and they are more subject to sandcracks. A sandcrack is a nasty, troublesome thing to cure. It is a crack which runs down the foot. It may not be necessarily the entire length of the foot, but inasmuch as such cracks usually commence from the coronet, which is the base of the horn growth, it must necessarily take a long time before it grows out.

As sandcracks are indicative of a weak foot, the growth of horn will probably be somewhat slower than in a healthy one, and it may be probably four or five months before it grows out. Where a sandcrack is a bad one, veterinary assistance must be procured; where but slight, a weak ointment of iodine, or some such preparation, occasionally rubbed into the coronet, will help to stimulate and promote the more rapid growth of horn. There are many horses which, when ridden, invariably suffer from sandcracks, but which will go in harness and keep sound.

Sandcrack may be caused by an injury to the coronet, such as a cut or tread. In such cases, though the same care and treatment is necessary, still the same anxiety need not be felt, since it by no means follows, unless the injury be very severe, that the horse will be likely to suffer from another, as would be the case if it had arisen from weakness of feet. Where a horse is naturally predisposed to suffer from them, the best plan is to sell him, unless he can be utilized for harness work alone, and will stand sound under such work.

Hoof-ointment may be used with advantage where horses suffer from weak or brittle feet. Glycerine is good, but it is rather expensive for stable use. What is called 'veterinary vaseline' is good and cheap enough. The mixture sold under the dreadfully long name of 'Hoplemuroma' is excellent, but it is by no means inexpensive; yet I think, where it is necessary, it is worth the price asked for it.

Prevention is better than cure. Horses are subject to many ailments, but considering the risks they run, and the gross neglect and mismanagement they often undergo, it becomes a matter for surprise, not how *many* these ailments are, but rather how few. Much can be prevented by the exercise of ordinary care and common-sense. Cleanliness in every detail connected with a stable will go very far towards the prevention of disease; without it, all other efforts are unavailing.

PART IV.

AILMENTS AND THEIR TREATMENT.

CHAPTER XX.

Mud fever.—Cold and cough.—Treatment.—Strangles.—Treatment.—Glanders and farcy.—Roaring and broken wind.—Roaring and whistling.—New cure for roaring.—Broken wind. — Treatment. — Wind-sucking and crib-biting. — Weaving. — String-halt. — Worms. — Bots. — Muzzles.—Tearing clothing.—Kicking in stable.—Capped hock.—Capped elbow.—Cracked heels.—Windgalls.—Spavin.—Thoroughpin.—Curb.—Ring-bone. — Side-bones. — Splint. —' Periosteotomy.' — Speedy-cut. — Navicular disease.—Sore backs and galls.—Sitfast.—Lampas.—Toothache.—' High-blowing.'—Ringworm.—Preparation for physic.—How to give a ball.—Physic after grass.—Purging.—Diseases of the eye.—Causes of blindness.—Blind coach-horses.

THE last chapter was devoted specially to shoeing and to the feet generally. I propose now to refer to some of the evils which horseflesh is liable to.

What is termed 'mud fever' is a comparatively modern ailment, and I can remember the time when such a thing was never heard of. Of late years it has become so common that I suppose there is not a hunting stable in the kingdom which has not at one time or other suffered from it in a greater or less degree. It is a somewhat troublesome thing to cure when contracted. However, I trust I may be able to show what is the cause of mud fever, or at least to explain how it may be prevented. I wonder how many miles of correspondence have been written on this subject? Certainly a great deal of nonsense and some little sense. All sorts of preparations have been made to cure it, but very few people appear to know how to prevent it. *I* did not until I was told, and since I found that the advice given me was good, I will give the reader the benefit of it.

The winter of 1872 was about as wet as any I can remember either before or since. Every day it rained more or less, generally more. Hunting was rather a misery than a pleasure. If hounds found and 'got away,' the 'going' was so heavy that horses were pulled to pieces, and nearly every stable I knew was more or less *hors de combat* from mud fever. I was at the time quartered at the cavalry depôt at Canterbury. One day, when conversing with our veterinary surgeon, the—I regret to say—late Mr. Longman, as good a sportsman, companion, and practitioner as ever lived, he remarked to me, 'What a number of horses have got mud fever! Yours have got it, I see, also. Now look at mine; *they* have not got it, and never do get it.' On my inquiring further on the subject, he gave me the following advice: '*Never wash a horse's legs when he comes in from hunting.* Dry them as well as you can, and brush every particle of dirt you can off them; then bandage them. An hour or so afterwards remove the bandages, and again brush and clean them. Put on fresh bandages, and the next day, after another good grooming, you *may*, if you like, then wash them. Should a horse come in *very* early from hunting, his legs *may* be washed, but not for several hours after, and after they have been dried and bandaged, as I have described; and even under these circumstances it is *better* not to wash them the same day.'

I followed his advice, and have never but once since then ever had the slightest *touch* of mud fever in my stable, and that once was when my groom confessed to me that he had disregarded my orders, and had washed the legs after hunting, and he added, 'I will never do it again'—a promise he very faithfully kept.

Whatever mud fever may be *said* to proceed from—and all sorts of causes have, as I have said, been assigned for it—the above is the way to *prevent* it, and it is simple enough. I could say a great deal more regarding it, but I do not think anything further than this is *necessary*, nor do I wish to bore the reader with a long-winded treatise on the subject. I only counsel him to follow the advice I had given to *me*, and to insist upon its being carried out. If so, he, at all events, will not be troubled with it in his stable.

Cold and cough is another great trouble. When it gets into a stable it is almost sure to run through it, and the result is that all the horses are down at once. They lose their condition, and the owner loses his sport or the use of them. A cold with a horse is by no means an ailment to be lightly treated. It *may* be very serious. A horse suffers infinitely more with a cold than we do, far more than people are apt to suppose; and it takes weeks, and often months, for a horse to completely recover from the effects of a cold which has been neglected at first, and very often when he does recover, he is unsound.

Generally speaking, a horse does not catch cold from exposure; it is rather from want of fresh, pure air, as I endeavoured to show at the commencement of this book. True it is that it does not do to let a horse which is clipped or sweating stand about in cold weather. He will very probably get chilled, and a cold be the result. With mankind a cold generally (at all events very often) is followed by a cough; with a horse the cough generally precedes the cold. A horse coughs, and the groom declares it to be 'nothing but a little stable cough.' A stable cough! The description would be better rendered as a *hot stable* cough. In such a case it is *more* than probable that, there being an utter absence of proper ventilation in the stable, the impure, vitiated air had irritated the mucous membrane, and so caused the cough. The irritation, unless treated promptly, spreads, and a cold is the result. The horse gets dull and listless, refuses his corn, and all the several stages of a bad cold ensue. The nostrils discharge; the poor horse is perfectly wretched. The owner is obliged to walk, and has to pay a veterinary surgeon a probably long bill, and all for the want of a little attention to proper ventilation.

It is, however, quite possible to stop a cold, if it is promptly treated. At the first symptom of a cough, if mustard is rubbed well into the throat, any further evil will probably be averted. The horse should also be put on laxative diet for a day or two, such as bran or linseed mashes. Should the cough run on into a settled cold, the horse should be at once removed to a large airy loose-box.

Steaming the head will relieve the animal. The best way of doing this is by half filling a bucket with hay, and pouring boiling water on it, in sufficient quantity to be nearly all absorbed by the hay, and the bucket should be held under the horse's head. This should be done two or three times a day. The diet should be laxative. Such corn (and it should be but little) as is given should be scalded, and everything done to prevent the increase of any feverish symptoms; a few carrots, or anything of the kind, may also be advantageously used.

Almost every young horse has what is called 'strangles,' and the sooner they have it and get over it the better. It may be termed an infantile complaint, although it is by no means uncommon for horses of mature age to have it, and horses *may* have it more than once, though it is somewhat exceptional for them to do so.

The treatment for strangles is much the same as for colds.

In strangles the glands of the throat, under the jaw, become very much enlarged. It is satisfactory when they burst outwardly, and suppurate *well*. If so, a horse is less liable to contract the complaint at any future time. As I have before remarked, young horses, on first coming into stables from grass, are almost certain to get it—and it is better not to check it. Where it is possible, a horse so affected should always be put into a box by himself, and away from other horses. Plenty of warm clothing and plenty of fresh, pure air is the best remedy. The disease must run its course.

Where strangles has been *very* severe, or where proper suppuration has not taken place, it is possible that a horse may turn a 'roarer;' but this is not, luckily, a very common termination of the disease, and under ordinary circumstances, and with the exercise of ordinary care, should be avoided.

I will not refer to the subject of glanders or farcy, further than to express my very earnest hope that the reader may never be unfortunate enough to have a horse afflicted with either. But *should* such be his ill-luck, I would urge him, as soon as it is pronounced beyond doubt, not to hesitate for an instant in giving orders for the destruction of his horse, even if the latter were 'worth a king's ransom'—and this in the interests of his neighbours as well as his own. Where such disease has been in a stable, that stable is never again really safe for a horse—to speak plainly, I do not believe that anything short of razing it to the ground, and replacing the soil whereon the stable has stood with entirely fresh, can be relied upon as being a thoroughly certain preventive against its recurrence at some future time. I do not think that I have at all over-estimated the extreme malignity of the disease. Every stitch of clothing, rug, brush, bucket, sponge—in fact, every article which has been used for or near to a glandered horse—should be burnt, as, I may also add, the very clothing of the groom who attended upon the horse. Attendance upon a glandered horse is fraught with extreme risk, and should a man unhappily contract it, there is little or no hope of saving him from a painful and horrible death. I have not, therefore, I think, over-estimated its danger.

I would impress upon the reader that what is called 'roaring' and what is termed 'broken-wind' are not one and the same thing, although numberless people cannot, apparently, distinguish between them.

Roaring is caused by paralysis of the cords of the throat. The nerve being paralyzed, the muscle is useless, and, ceasing to act, becomes an impediment, and is therefore incapable of expansion and contraction. The noise is produced during the process of inhalation, and not that of exhalation. The muscle gets in the way, as it were. The disease increases as time goes on.

'Whistling' is none other than incipient roaring.

All kinds of treatment have been tried from time

to time, such as blistering, firing, galvanism, etc., but without any good and satisfactory results. I am informed that there is a doctor living at Bicester who has discovered an operation by which a cure can be effected, and I am assured that the cure is complete. If this is the case—and I have every reason to credit my informant—it will prove a boon to many a horse-owner.

Since writing the foregoing I have, through a friend, been placed in communication with the gentleman referred to: viz., Dr. Cotterell, living at Bicester, and in answer to my queries on the subject, he replied most kindly and fully, and gave me, at my request, his sanction to make any use of his letters which I might desire. And as it may interest some of my readers, I will quote such portions as may be necessary. He writes:

'Regarding my operation for roaring, after a large and varied experience, I find that one can certainly improve by my operation (not do away with the noise), and thus increase the staying powers of a horse up to six years old; but after that age, owing to calcification of the arytenoid cartilages, the removal of the left cartilage, together with the corresponding false and true vocal cords, gives the best result.

'My operation consists essentially in removing

the whole of the anterior process and vocal process of the left arytenoid cartilage, together with true and false vocal cords, the laryngeal sinus and the cartilage of Santorini on the same side. All this must be done through an opening in the inter-thyroid membrane, and the cricoid cartilage should not be divided. If done in old horses, there is a large mass of granulation material formed where the anterior process is separated from the body of the arytenoid cartilage, due to calcification of the cartilage ; hence removal of entire cartilage is best in these cases.

'The principal advantages of my operation over the total extirpation of the cartilage, as practised by Möller, Fleming, and others, are :

'1. The posterior wall of the larynx is left intact with a resistant cartilage, as in health, giving rise to less likelihood of food, water, etc., getting into the lungs, and thus causing inflammation and death.

'2. The insertion of the left lateral crico-thyroid muscle is not interfered with, and it is only in very advanced and old cases of roaring that this muscle ceases entirely to act, consequently the muscle still retains a certain power of swinging open the left side of the larynx.'

Too tight reining or neglected cold will produce

roaring. I have observed that horses whose necks are very long, and those which are over-thick and coarse in the neck, are more subject to contract the disease. In the latter case, tight-reining and being forced to carry their heads in a manner for which their shape is not adapted is probably the cause.

Broken-wind is brought on sometimes by a neglected cold; at others, by a horse being galloped too soon after feeding or watering. It is caused from the covering of the air-cells becoming ruptured, and the air thereby entering into other cells, cannot be expelled from them without very great exertion of the muscles. The air-cells may also themselves become run into each other. There is absolutely no cure, but careful and moderate feeding will very much help to relieve it. Feeding little and often with good and digestible food, and care in watering, is also necessary (but little water being allowed at a time). A horse so affected should never be worked soon after feeding or watering.

Wind-sucking and crib-biting may be called first-cousins. The latter leads to the former. A disordered stomach is usually the cause, produced generally by idleness and over-feeding.

They may be prevented by the use of a crib-biting strap, which has an iron tongue covered with leather and padded, which is strapped round the throat. The tongue, being at right angles to the strap, and under the throat and jaw, prevents a horse from getting his head down. In this position he can neither suck wind nor crib-bite.

They are *said* to be infectious—that horses catch the habit from each other. This I do not believe; and, indeed, my own personal experience points to the contrary. In every troop of cavalry in the service there is sure to be at *least* one horse which is either a wind-sucker or a crib-biter. The *other* horses do not contract the habit, so that it *cannot* be catching. I can, however, quite understand how the idea has arisen that it *is* so.

As I have recently remarked, both habits are the result of a disordered state of stomach, and indigestion, etc. Now, it is quite possible that in a stable where one horse is suffering from the combined ill effects of over-feeding and under-working, the others may be suffering in like manner in a greater or less degree. The horse which is most delicately constituted is the first victim, and is therefore the first to acquire the habit. The others, being more or less in a similar condition, very readily catch it from him. If this were *not* so, how could troop-horses, which are separated from each other by 'bails' only, fail to acquire the habit from one or more of their comrades which may be confirmed in it? If over-feeding and idleness will produce it in *one* horse, it is surely but reasonable only to presume that they will do so in the case of another.

'Weaving' has nothing to do with either of the two former vices, and is simply a nervous affection. A horse rarely 'weaves' when he is not sensible of being observed. It is a sort of St. Vitus' dance. It does no harm to the horse. Some of the best horses will 'weave.' It is annoying to an observer. It is no more than an unceasing swinging to and fro of the head from side to side. It appears to be more common in well-bred horses than in others. Horses which 'weave' rarely carry high condition. They are generally of a highly-strung nervous temperament, and their very nervousness prevents their putting on much flesh.

String-halt, a peculiar catching up of the leg (generally the hind-leg), is another nervous disease, if disease it may be termed. It is no detriment to a horse unless it is *very* bad. It seems to be confined chiefly to horses of the same temperament and class as those which I have described as 'weavers.' It generally ceases directly a horse gets into his work, and in no way affects his galloping or jumping.

There is no *known* cure for it. If I were buying a horse and he were but *slightly* string-halt, I should not any the less buy him if I were otherwise satisfied with him. On the contrary, I often think that string-halt is indicative of good quality and pluck, and certainly some of the best horses I have ever known across country have been string-halt. I think, however, that it does not decrease, but rather increases, with age. Nobody has as yet been able to assign the exact cause which produces it, though there must, of course, be a cause.

Worms are a trouble which can easily be got rid of, and the sooner they are the better. It is an easy matter to tell when a horse has worms. His skin is dry, his coat stares, he rubs his tail, loses condition, and looks altogether thriftless and rusty. Such conditions indicate the presence of worms.

The cure is one I quote from the best authority, viz. : Two drachms of sulphate of iron mixed up in a little wet bran, and given, fasting, the first thing every morning for a fortnight. This may be followed by a mild dose of physic.

I have read, and I believe the statement, that worms, being bloodless animals, cannot thrive in the stomach of a healthy horse—that their very presence indicates a lack of blood in the system, and the latter is still *further* weakened by their presence. The sulphate of iron is a blood-forming tonic. As the stomach recovers its proper tone the worms die. The physic clears them out.

There are two or three different kinds of worms to which horses are subject. As the treatment is the same for all, I need not go further into the matter here than to remark that those which are termed 'bots' (and which come from the gadfly), are the most troublesome, inasmuch as they fix themselves into the coats of the stomach.

It is possible that horses take them in when at grass, or that they may come with the use of green forage. The coats of horses at grass are often covered with little yellow lumps. These are supposed to be the eggs of the gadfly, and it is asserted that horses, in licking their coats, swallow these eggs, and that they hatch inside their stomachs, and so they suffer from bots. This may or may not be the case. I only mention it as being an accepted theory by many persons, and I have no reason to *doubt* it.

Some horses have an unfortunate habit of eating their bedding, and blow themselves out to an extent which militates very much against their being kept in condition for work. There are only two ways of preventing this: the one, by putting them on bedding which they cannot eat, such as sawdust, etc.; the other, by the use of a muzzle. The former is, in my opinion, the better plan, as I dislike muzzling a horse if it can possibly be avoided.

As I omitted to make mention of muzzles in the chapter on saddlery, I may here state that they are made both of leather and wire. If the former, they should be lined with tin. Their price is about 10s. 6d.

There are, again, horses which persistently tear their clothing; and a very expensive and annoying habit it is. It proceeds from itchiness of skin, or worms. They may be prevented doing any damage by means of a shield of stout leather, which is made to buckle on to the back strap of the noseband of the headstall, and long enough to reach to the bottom of the under-jaw. It is a very simple arrangement, which any saddler can construct. Horses which kick in the stable (and some horses are most inveterate kickers, often damaging themselves very seriously) generally suffer from capped hocks; that is to say, the point of the hock gets thickened and enlarged, and is very unsightly; in extremely bad cases matter will form, and a running sore ensue. It is a difficult matter to prevent this habit at times. Such kicking generally takes place at night, and is, besides being very damaging to the horse, an intolerable nuisance to the inhabitants of any houses which may be near. Shackles *may* prevent it, but as a rule, if a horse means kicking, he will manage it somehow or other, and kick shackles and all. Being much troubled in this way by one of my own horses, my groom very ingeniously contrived the following arrangement, which answered so admirably that I will give the reader the benefit of it: He fastened two buckets of water every night to the pillar-rein of the stall, just at such a height that when the horse kicked the water splashed over him. He very soon gave up the trick, and never kicked so long as the buckets were there.

Capped hock of any standing cannot be quite got rid of. The best plan is frequent hand-rubbing. A *very mild* solution of bichloride of mercury is, I have been told, efficacious, but it must be very mild, and should be applied with a cork, the same way as the hair, *i.e.*, *with* the hair, and not rubbed *against* it. Pressure may also serve to reduce it, but no very great results must be expected if the cartilage has become much thickened.

Capped elbow, which is a thickening of the cap of the elbow, is also as troublesome, if not as unsightly, as capped hock. I have seen horses whose elbows have been so enlarged as to be of the size of a large orange, and dripping with matter. In such cases there is nothing for it but to have them removed by excision. It is commonly and ignorantly supposed that capped elbow is caused by the toe of the hind-foot rubbing against the elbow when a horse is lying down. This is altogether wrong. It is really caused by the heel of the shoe which is on the foot of the leg itself of which the elbow is capped. It is true it is done when the horse is lying down, but the shoe of the *hind* foot has nothing whatever to do with it. Capped elbow is rarely found in other than big, heavy horses, whose feet are large and whose shoes are heavy, especially amongst cart and big carriage horses.

It is very easily prevented by the use of a leather bolster stuffed well with horsehair, and provided with a buckle at one end and a strap at the other, and made long enough to fit round the fetlock. It should be made circular, and should be sufficiently large in diameter, so that when a horse is lying down it is thick enough to keep the heel of the shoe well away from the elbow. It answers most perfectly. If prevention is better than cure, in the present instance it is most certainly *half way* to it, and when once you have stopped the evil, it is possible to reduce the enlargement.

I have before made mention of cracked heels,

their cause and their prevention, and I now give the following recipe for their cure, viz.: Wash thoroughly with soft-soap and lukewarm water, and then apply the following lotion, viz.: One part of chloride of zinc, twenty parts of water.

Wind-galls are more of a blemish than an actual unsoundness. Their presence is rather indicative of an excess of lubricating oil. They appear above and around the fetlock-joints, and are round, puffy-looking lumps. They are soft, and yield to the pressure of the hand. Hand-rubbing and bandaging and blistering will help to reduce them, but they generally recur with hard work. I was told by a farrier, who was serving at the forge of the cavalry depot at Canterbury, that he, acting under instructions, endeavoured to effect a cure on a horse which was very much wind-galled by daily hand-rubbing, and kneading the wind-galls until they were gradually forced into one. A seton was then applied, and the oily deposit allowed to exude. He informed me that it answered very well for a time; but that when the horse was again put to work they formed as before. I cannot but think myself that it is best to leave them alone, and to endeavour to keep them down by hand-rubbing and bandaging only. Probably, if a horse subject to them had *not* got them, he would not last as long.

Spavins are of three kinds, viz. : bog, blood, and bone spavins. The first is due to enlargement of the mucous sacs between the tendons of the hock on its inside. The second is caused by the former, which, being excessive, distends the vein which passes over it. Such spavins do not always cause lameness ; but when they do, blistering or firing must be resorted to. The latter is the more efficacious. Bone spavin is a deposit of bony matter on the joint of the hock. It almost invariably occurs on its inner and lower side. At times the deposit may take place between the smaller bones of the hock ; but in either case a horse is generally more or less lame, and I regret to add that there is no cure but firing.

Horses with very straight hocks are more liable to bog and blood spavins than those whose hocks are more bent.

Thoroughpin may be described as a wind-gall in the hock, between the muscle and tendon. It can be reduced by means of a truss, which clasps it on both sides of the hock. Thoroughpin does not necessarily cause lameness—indeed, but comparatively seldom.

Curb occurs at the back of the hock, and is recognised by a swelling caused by the strain of the tendon, or the sheath of the tendon or of its enveloping ligament. Slight curbs do not necessarily cause lameness, but, as a rule, all curbs do so more or less. The firing-iron is the only permanent cure. Blistering may reduce them and help to strengthen the hocks, but the effect is not equal to that of firing. Horses with overbent and weak hocks are most subject to them. In Ireland it is a common practice to fire young horses whose hocks are at all faulty, whether they are sound or not, merely as a preventive. It may be a wise thing to do, but it always seems to me very much like pulling out a sound tooth for fear it should decay.

Ring-bone is a deposit of bony matter on the cartilage surrounding the coronet. The formation is the result of concussion, and is attended with considerable heat and lameness. When taken in the early stage, blistering may cure it, but, as a rule, firing is necessary. Good shoeing and *light* shoes will help to prevent its recurrence.

As I observed in the chapter on shoeing, side-bone is the ossification of the cartilage attached to the wings of the coffin-bone. Horses with short, stumpy pasterns are more liable to side-bones than those with longer and more springy pasterns. Side-bones do not cause lameness as a rule, but the elasticity of a horse's action—the tread — is reduced. They may be successfully treated, if taken in time, by blistering or firing. A horse subject to them may be reasonably suspected of being disposed to contract ring-bone, and careful shoeing, as for ring-bone, is therefore advisable.

Splint is of very common occurrence. There are, in fact, but very few horses which have been subjected to hard work, especially roadwork, which are perfectly free from it. It is a deposit of bony matter on the bone of the leg, invariably on the fore-leg, and nearly always on its inner side. It is generally caused by the irritation set up by concussion. As in the case of a broken limb, a certain amount of inflammation is necessary, in order that fresh bone, or what answers to bone (viz., callus), may be thrown out for the purpose of uniting the fractured bone; so undue irritation, causing inflammation, brings about a superfluous deposit on the sound limb, and thereby renders it unsound. This deposit being lodged between the bone itself and the skin, or, as it is termed, the periosteum which covers it, causes severe pain and lameness. If the deposit is lodged well forward on the leg so as not to implicate what are termed the 'splint-bones' themselves, or to interfere with the action of the tendons, or so placed as not to be struck by the foot of the other leg, it does not much matter, and is only a blemish; but where either the splint-bones or tendons are interfered with the case is different, and the offending deposit must be removed. Rest, light food, and cold-water bandaging is the first step necessary, in order to reduce the inflammation as speedily as possible, and this must be followed by blistering. Where a splint is not badly placed, I would advise the reader to leave it alone; the very remedy itself might make matters worse. There *is* an operation for splint which I have known and proved to be very successful. It is termed periosteotomy. I will explain it. Although the *distension* of the periosteum is excessively painful, it (the periosteum) may be cut without any very great pain being inflicted. The operation is thus performed : The skin of the leg is moved round by the hand from the back of the leg, as far as it *can* be so done, until it is over the splint. A downward incision is then made through the skin and periosteum on to the very splint itself. The splint is thus at once freed, and so is the periosteum from any distension. The pain is relieved, and the slit which has been made in the skin soon heals, as it is not over the lump formed by the splint. By the time the periosteum has grown again it has adapted itself to the form of the splint. Young horses, whose bones are not fully matured and are soft, are very liable to splint. Big, heavy horses also are always more subject to it than lighter horses.

Splint may be also caused by a blow, or anything which may cause inflammation. Horses whose toes turn in, who are what is termed 'pigeon-toed,' are apt to get them on the outer side of the leg, inasmuch as the weight comes more on that side than on the inner, as is the case with properly formed horses. The better the quality of the bone, and the more matured it is, the less liable it is to throw out splint.

Speedy-cut is caused by the foot of one leg striking against the other leg. It occurs under the knee-joint. High-stepping horses whose action is not perfectly true are liable to it. It may be caused by bad shoeing, but proper shoeing will prevent it. I have in my possession at the present time one of the very best ponies in England. When I bought her some five years ago she had the marks of being *very badly* speedy-cut. Doubtless it was caused by bad shoeing, as her action is, though very high, as true and just as it could be, and she has never once touched herself since I bought her. I have always had her shod with ordinary shoes, very much of the Fitzwygram pattern. The treatment for speedy-cut is the same as for splint.

Navicular may be termed an incurable disease, for there is no cure for it. I say so sadly, for I have known some of the very best of good horses fall victims to it. When speaking of the bones of the foot, at the commencement of the chapter on shoeing, I remarked on a small, curiously-shaped bone which is situated at the back of the coffin and smaller pastern bones. This is the navicular bone. Over this bone the ligament which connects the bones of the fore-leg and foot passes. It is between this ligament and the navicular bone that the seat of this disease lies. The latter may be caused by either a strain of the ligament, which, becoming inflamed, sets up ulceration of the bone ; or it may be that a sudden jerk or wrench may cause the ulceration. I believe that it is very much a matter of doubt which of the two is the cause— that is to say, whether the bone is ulcerated by contact with the affected ligament or not. Be that as it may, the bone becomes diseased, and there is no known treatment which will arrest it. The pain may be got rid of by a painful operation—viz., 'nerving' or 'unnerving,' as it is sometimes called— but it does not stop the disease, and sooner or later there is nothing for it but to destroy the animal. It is beyond doubt very much hereditary, as there are some strains of blood which are more predisposed to it than others, and it has been traced back for generations of the same blood.

In ordinary diseases of the foot, the diseased foot is generally the hottest of the two ; with navicular disease this is *not* the case. It is a peculiarity of this disease that the affected foot is generally the coldest—indeed, at times icily cold—but the temperature very seldom remains constant for any length of time, and a foot so affected may be at one time icy cold, and within a few minutes equally hot. The presence of navicular disease is generally indicated by a horse pointing his leg out in the stable, for the purpose, it may be presumed, of relaxing the pressure of the ligament on the bone. Whenever a horse so stands in the stable it is to be regarded with great suspicion.

Whenever doubt may arise as to which is the diseased foot, if *both* feet are wetted simultaneously, and one is seen to dry more rapidly than the other, it may be assumed that the one which remains wet the longest is the one affected. When a horse contracts the disease in one foot, the other foot generally follows suit, probably from sympathy. It is better to continue to work a horse in the first stages of the ailment, as work promotes the circulation, and a horse will often work perfectly sound though suffering from navicular disease, and for a considerable period at times, according as it is slow or rapid in its progress. However, as I have remarked, there is nothing for it for either horse or owner but to grin and bear it. Navicular disease does not seem to confine itself to any one class of horse more than another. Perhaps wellbred horses are more subject to it; if so, it may be assumed that the nature of their work is more likely to produce it, especially if predisposed to it.

As I have observed in my remarks on saddle-fitting, a sore back is a thing to be avoided, and this it may be by the use of a well-fitting saddle and good riding. A sore back not only takes a long time to heal properly, but it is very liable to recur unless thoroughly treated, and due time allowed to elapse before any pressure is put upon it. The same applies to a shoulder which has been wrung by the collar.

After work a horse's back should be always carefully examined, and any damp-looking or tender spots should be at once taken notice of. If the skin has only 'risen,' the application of what is called by laundresses a 'blue-bag' will be found very beneficial. The place only requires to be well dabbed with it for a day or two. After that it should be well sponged with salt and water twice a day; but care should be taken that when this is done all the salt should be well brushed out of the hair before a saddle is again used, or otherwise the crystals of the salt will establish a raw very rapidly. The salt water is used only for the purpose of hardening the skin. If the skin is broken, it should be first bathed with warm water, and then one of the following applied, viz. : Glycerine and tannin, spermaceti ointment, or Holloway's ointment. I pin my faith on the latter. The glycerine and tannin is, perhaps, more speedy, but not so good, if proper time for cure can be given. Of course a horse must not be worked with a sore back, unless the saddle is 'chambered,' as I have before described. When the skin has *quite* healed, and the hair begins to grow again, the salt and water may be used.

It is by no means an uncommon occurrence to find what is called a 'sitfast' on the back of a horse. It has been caused by the horse's back having been sore, and not properly treated. It is, in fact, a corn in the back. Needless to say, when a horse has a sitfast, his back is very prone to gall on the slightest provocation. May I urge the reader, if he should ever possess a horse with a sitfast, to adopt the following plan, viz. : sponge the back with warm water daily, and rub on some Holloway's ointment, and also, having placed some of it on a piece of brown paper or rag, fasten it, as best he can, so as to keep it on the sitfast? Repeat the washing and the ointment daily for several days. It may be necessary to do so for a week or ten days, according to the depth of the corn. At the end of that time the sitfast can be pulled out with a pair of forceps, and if the above treatment has been properly adhered to, every root will come away with it. As these roots are at times of considerable length, it is necessary to foment and apply the ointment well round the sitfast for some two or three inches. The place will heal very rapidly, and will not easily become sore again. This is a mode of treating a sitfast which is always successful, and one, simple as it is, which is not generally known.

Lampas is a swelling of the roof of the mouth, and very much interferes with a horse's feeding. It is more general with young horses during the period of their teething, but is by no means confined to them alone, as those of mature age are subject to it at times. A dose of physic, or even a few days' laxative diet, will generally cure it, if slight, but in extreme cases it may be necessary to lance the edges of the palate. As soon as this is done, the horse will at once be able to feed.

Whenever a horse is off his feed, it is well to examine the roof of his mouth to see if lampas is the cause. It is a very simple and easy thing to cure.

Toothache may produce lampas; horses suffer more from toothache than is supposed. There is no cure for it but removal of the tooth, which is a somewhat difficult business, and very often not by any means performed as gently as it might be.

High-blowing is often mistaken for defective wind. It is, on the contrary, indicative of extra good wind. The noise made by a high-blower proceeds from the nostrils only, which latter flap, as it were, during the process of exhalation. A high-blower is really more valuable than a horse which is not.

Ringworm at times gets into a stable. It is contagious, but is easily cured by the application of some strong astringent. A solution of copperas, rubbed on, will answer. Common ink will do if nothing else is at hand.

Whenever it is required to give a horse physic, it is necessary that he should be 'prepared,' as it is termed, to receive it. Without due preparation, not only is the proper action of the medicine very much weakened, but instead of doing good, it is quite possible to do harm. The preparing a horse for physic consists in keeping him on sloppy branmashes for twenty-four hours previously. It might at first sight, perhaps, be considered a waste of time, this twenty-four hours' preparation. Such is not the case, however, inasmuch as the medicine, acting more thoroughly, acts also more quickly, and recovery is therefore more speedy.

Every groom should know how, and be able, to give a physic ball; but if he does not, it is better to leave it to a competent person. The way to give a ball is this: The horse's head must be raised, and for this purpose it is necessary for the person giving the ball to stand on a stool or on a stable-bucket. Having wetted or greased the ball, which latter should be held between the tips of the fingers of the left hand by its end, the horse's mouth having been opened, his tongue should be seized firmly by the right hand and brought round on the near side of his mouth as far back as can be. The hand holding the ball is then thrust down the horse's throat as far as it can reach, the ball being placed lengthwise in the throat. The hand being withdrawn as soon as the ball is properly lodged, the tongue is released, and the horse's head kept still raised, until the passage of the ball down the throat can be seen, as can easily be done if the outside of the throat is carefully watched. A drink of chilled water should be then given. The following morning the horse may be gently walked about for a short time to encourage the action of the physic. It is a good plan to physic horses mildly when first coming up from grass, etc., and I am convinced that by so doing they are more easily and quickly got into condition.

Excessive purging may be stopped by giving a little oatmeal gruel, or, if that fails, gruel made of wheaten flour or a little dry bran. If these fail, the advice of a veterinary surgeon had better be procured; but it is unwise to interfere with purging unless it *is excessive*.

Horses are subject to diseases of the eye, such as ophthalmia, cataract, etc. I will only, however, remark on the latter of these—cataract—as it is the one most frequently met with, and is far more common than it should be, since I am convinced that more than half of the horses which suffer from cataract are victims to the carelessness of servants. Seven times out of ten it is the result of a blow or some gross carelessness. I may as well at once state that cataract is well-nigh incurable. A horse's eye cannot be operated on easily. It *can* be done, but it is a matter of extreme difficulty to do so.

Horses which are hard driven are subject to the disease. I have been told that in the old coaching days nearly half the coach-horses were blind, evidently from the pressure of the collar and being forced to travel at a high rate of speed to keep time. Hence, perhaps, the old coaching phrase, 'Three blind 'uns and a bolter.' Within half a mile of the place where I am sitting as I write this is a field in which in those days the horses belonging to a then well-known coach proprietor were turned out to grass. I have been told, by the most unquestionable authority, that more than half of them were partially or totally blind.

Blind horses rarely stumble or fall. I suppose that their other senses are sharpened by their loss of sight, and they are careful also to raise their feet clear of the ground. A horse's eye is *very* easily knocked out. I often wonder that their eyes are not more frequently damaged than they are, from the rough and ruthless manner in which grooms thrust the collars over their heads.

It is very difficult for an amateur to detect a cataract in its primary stages, and it requires the skill of a practical veterinary surgeon to do so. The best way to examine the sight of a horse is to put him into a darkened stable, and inspect it by the light of a candle.

CHAPTER XXI.

Recipe for physic-balls.—Recipe for cleaning leather breeches.—Recipe for cleaning white cords.—Recipe for cleaning brown cords.—Recipe for cleaning top-boots.—Recipe for cleaning scarlet coats.—Recipe for cleaning drab-coats.—Recipe for cleaning hunting-hats.

The following recipes may be of use to the reader :

PHYSIC BALL FOR A 15.2 HORSE.

Best Barbadoes aloes	$2\frac{1}{2}$ drs.
Calomel . . .	10 grs.
Tartar emetic . .	15 ,,
Ground ginger . .	1 dr.

FOR A 16-HAND HORSE.

Aloes	3 drs.
Calomel . . .	12 grs.
Tartar emetic .	16 ,,
Ground ginger .	$1\frac{1}{4}$ drs.

To CLEAN LEATHER BREECHES.

Scour the breeches with a brush dipped in *clean*, soft water, but do not make them too wet. Then apply some of the following mixture :

Prepared chalk	8 oz.
Alum . . .	4 ,,

RECIPES.

Isinglass	.	$\frac{1}{2}$ oz.
Powdered pumice-stone	.	1 ,,
White soap .	.	2 ,,
Pipeclay	.	3 cakes.
Starch	.	1 tablespoonful.
Sweet oil .	.	6 ,,

Mix with boiling water to the consistency of thick cream, and apply lightly with a brush. Let the leathers dry slowly and thoroughly, and then dust them well with a cane; next, stretch them to their proper size on the trees, and then iron with a box-iron, taking care not to scorch them.

I may add that, when *cleaning* the breeches, should any stain of mud not readily come out, the use of a little lemon-juice will be found useful; but it should be washed out again with water.

To Clean White Cotton Cords.

Wash the breeches in very hot soapy water (soft water is best), and then rinse them in clean water. Dry before the fire, and when dry rub them well with a towel, in order to raise the pile again.

To Clean Brown Cotton Cords.

Peel and scrape 5 or 6 raw potatoes to a pulp into a basin, and then cover the pulp with rainwater, and let it stand for nearly an hour.

Strain off the pulp, and scour the cords well with a water-brush dipped in the liquid, and dry them before the fire, and not in the sun. When dry, rub well with a rough towel to raise the pile.

I took the above recipe from the *Field* many years ago, and have invariably used it ever since, as it is so thoroughly good. Brown cords when washed in the ordinary way lose their colour, but treated as above their colour never changes.

To Clean White Tops.

Dissolve 1 oz. of white copperas in a bottleful of rainwater, and add to it 1 oz. of oxalic acid. Apply this solution to the tops with a sponge; brush up and down.

For any other coloured tops, Propert's Powder is the best preparation.

To Clean Scarlet Coats.

A preparation for this purpose is, or used to be, sold by Messrs. Truefitt, in the Burlington Arcade. It is applied with a short, stiff brush (a toothbrush answers the purpose), and *dabbed* on the coat, not scrubbed. Mr. Cooper the saddler, in York, used to sell a similar preparation. I have no doubt but that it can be obtained elsewhere. It is a very useful preparation to have by one, as it so often happens that a new hunting coat gets stained with black mud, etc., and the stain will not come out properly.

A solution made of the following will be found also useful for the purpose of ordinary cleaning, whether of red or black coats, viz.:

> Liquor ammoniæ fortis, diluted with five times its quantity of water.

The coat should be well sponged with the above.

To Clean Drab Coats.

Coachmen's drab driving coats, and such coloured cloth, may be cleaned by using bran, rubbed well into the cloth. The cloth should be well brushed previously. If *very* dirty, the bran may be wetted, and the cloth finished up with plenty of dry bran.

To Clean a Hunting-Hat.

Brush it well with a hard brush, dipped in clean cold water, and then use a soft brush to finish with when dry. If the hat is *very* dull, about 2 drops of sweet oil placed on a *silk* handkerchief, and passed round the hat several times, will restore its appearance; but if more oil than this is used, it will give a sticky and over-shiny look.

I may as well caution the reader not to give his hat to a hatter to iron if it has been oiled. The hatter will scarcely feel grateful if he finds his irons and brushes spoiled by the oil on the hat.

CHAPTER XXII.

Livery.—Vulgar liveries.—Leather waist-belts.—Pad-grooms.
—Equipment for pad-grooms.—Riding-clothes.—Advice as
to the purchase of a horse.—Engagement-form for men-
servants.—Finale.

I PRESUME here to offer a few remarks on the subject of livery. As I observed at the commencement of this book, my intention in writing it is to benefit those who have little or no knowledge of the subjects of which I have treated. Hence advice which would perhaps be deemed an impertinence under other circumstances will, I trust, be accepted in the spirit in which it is intended.

In selecting livery for his servants, may I urge the reader to make choice of a colour, or combination of colours, which is unobtrusive and free from any appearance of flashiness? I am sure that his natural instincts as a gentleman will insure this being so; but one does at times see such truly fearful things in the way of livery, that it is well to avoid any possibility of being laughed at or thought vulgar.

If your means and establishment, generally, warrant it, special livery may and should be worn, otherwise a plain black or dark-blue coat is the most suitable, and without facings or fancy collars of any kind. For the country or on any but a full dress occasion, what can possibly look worse than servants with gold lace on their hats? It bespeaks either ignorance or vulgarity, or both. Nothing further should be worn than a plain black hat with a cockade, if the owner is entitled to wear it by reason of *actual* military or naval rank, or civil official position, and in these cases only. Why try to ape a rank which you have no right to? I have before me now the spectacle presented by the servants of a *nouveau riche* in a certain county, dressed up in all the magnificence of drab coats, magenta facings, and silver lace wherever lace can be put; and this is sported on all occasions.

Very frequently a gold-lace band, too often adorning a hat fit only for a scarecrow, is but the crowning glory to an ill-fitting and badly cleaned pair of breeches and gaiters, and the harness, horses, and whole turn-out generally are of a similar description. A carriage servant, *i.e.*, a coachman, should always be dressed in breeches and top-boots, and both should be made to fit him, and kept scrupulously clean. If top-boots are not worn, then plain black or very dark gray trousers should be used; but gaiters are not *de rigueur*. They savour of the market gardener, or of the man who cleans the pigs and pony, and does the odd jobs generally.

Let everything be in keeping. If the harness is of brass, the buttons of your livery must be gilt; if plated, they, too, must be plated. The metal fittings of your carriage and those of your harness and livery must all correspond.

It is attention to these little details which marks the well turned-out equipage. If it is but a pony-trap, let everything be as good, well fitting, and well cleaned as it can possibly be. I have many a time seen grooms wearing leather waist-belts when sitting at the back of a dog-cart. Such is absurd. The use of the belt arose from the old custom of the groom wearing a spare stirrup-leather when riding behind his master. What on earth, therefore, can be the use of a stirrup-leather in a dog-cart?

Grooms when riding behind a lady should be made to keep their proper distance of fifty yards, and should always be on the watch to be ready if required. Nothing can possibly look more disrespectful than to see a groom riding nearly alongside his mistress, and if he keeps too close behind his horse very frequently upsets the one she is riding.

I do not think that grooms should ever be allowed to wear spurs on horseback. They do not require them, and if they have not got them on they cannot misuse them. A pad-groom should carry a hunting-crop *without* a lash, as it is useful to open gates with.

And now may I venture to say a few words regarding the riding dress of the reader himself? Let it be plain and simple—severely so, if you will; but let breeches and boots, or trousers, or whatever may be worn, be made by a man who *can* make them. Do not let an otherwise smart and creditable turn-out be marred for the sake of a little extra trouble and expense. Messrs. Tautz and Sons or Messrs. Hammond will make you a pair of riding breeches or trousers as they should be made, and Messrs. Bartley or Peel, or other well-known London makers, will make your boots, etc. Thus attired, you need not fear criticism anywhere, go where you will. To be suitably attired is half-way to riding well and with comfort.

And now, ere I bring my little book to a close, I would add a few words of advice regarding the purchase of a horse:

Make up your mind exactly as to what kind of a horse you require—age, height, colour, etc. Go to a good dealer. If he shows you a horse which you like and which answers to what you require, *see him tried in every way you can before you try him yourself.* Do not listen too much to what the dealer says, and *never contradict* him. If you like the horse, and you think he will suit you, try him yourself. Inquire the price, and if that is also suitable, have him examined by the *very best* veterinary surgeon you can procure. A *good* dealer will not sell you a *bad* horse. He may be plain, he may be slow, he may be lots of things; but the chances are that he is sound, as far as he knows, and if not worth *all* the money he asks for him, he is, at all events, worth *some* of it. Never allow a dealer to talk you into buying a horse you do not like. If you do not like him, say so at once, and, if you can help it, do not assign any reason for saying so. Always talk as little as you can about horses when you are purchasing them. Talk of the weather, anything *else* you like; but if you don't know much about horses be as silent as you can. The dealer may probably imagine you know more than you really do. Remember the old adage, ' A still tongue makes a wise head.' When riding the horse before the dealer or grooms, try to forget their presence, and to think of nothing but the horse you are trying, and instantly check any attempts on their part, whether you are riding or not, to crack whips or rattle hats at the horse you are inspecting. If you purchase a horse, do not be disappointed when he comes home if he does not look as smart and big in *your* stable as he did in the dealer's, for it is part of a dealer's trade to make his horses look their *very best*, and your own groom will never succeed in making him look the same.

The following list of questions and form of engagement for servants may be found useful, especially in a large establishment. I have copied it from one in use. It contains columns for the following questions, and is printed:

Application for _____ situation.
In the employment of __

Name of Applicant
Present Address

Age.	Height.	Weight.	
If married.	Wife living.	No. of children.	Boys, with ages.	Girls, with ages.

General appearance

ENGAGEMENT-FORM.

Last situation, with employer's name _____

Address _____

Capacity.   Length of service.

_____

Reasons for leaving _____

_____

Previous situations.	Capacity.	Length of service.
1. _____	1. _____	1. _____
2. _____	2. _____	2. _____
3. _____	3. _____	3. _____

Application for character to
Address

How long out of employ.	When at liberty.	Religion.

⎰ Wages paid in last situation, ⎱ £ per annum.	Board wages paid in last situation, £ per week.
⎰ Wages to be paid if engaged, ⎱ £ per annum.	Board wages to be paid if engaged, £ per week.
⎰ Whether paid weekly, fort- ⎨ nightly, monthly or quar- ⎱ terly	Whether paid weekly, fortnightly, monthly or quarterly _____

⎰ Beer allowance per week, ⎱ 2s. or 2s. 6d.	Indoor Servants.
⎧ Travelling expenses for ⎪ journeys of 6 to 8 hours, ⎨ 2s. 6d. ; exceeding 8 hours, ⎪ maximum charge, 5s. per ⎩ diem.	Hair-powder, per quarter, 10s. Plate-powder, per quarter, 20s. Washing white waistcoats, per quarter, 20s. Pumps (if not supplied), per annum, 20s. Extras, if any

Liveries will be supplied when considered to be necessary, and belong to the employer. Servants leaving the employ are not at liberty to remove any portion of their livery or working suit without special permission.

Working suits are provided for *indoor* servants in livery once a year.

Working suits are provided for stablemen in livery twice a year.

Notice to quit to be one calendar month on either side, except in cases of misconduct, when the wages will only be paid up to the day of dismissal, and no railway or other expenses will be allowed.

Tradesmen's accounts are not to be contracted without orders. All orders to be sent through the order-book, and to receive the signature of the employer or his agent, before the goods can be delivered, and no perquisite can be allowed.

Remarks.

{ Signature of applicant _____ _____

{ Signature of employer, or his agent __ _____

Where interviewed _____

Date_____ , 18_____

On the *back* of the form :

Number____

MEN-SERVANTS' ENGAGEMENT-FORM.

Name.

Capacity.

Date of Engagement.

Date of Leaving.

Remarks.

In Whose Employ.

Where.

And now I will close my labour, which has been very much one of love. I trust that the foregoing may prove of some slight service to someone or other. If so, I shall have the satisfaction of feeling that, while the compilation of my little book has been a source of great pleasure and amusement to me, during the long hours of the winter evenings, I shall also have not been utterly without some use in the world.

If at any time a possible reader of the foregoing pages may wish for further information which it is in my power to give him (and I have purposely kept as free as I could from any long-winded dissertations on any of the subjects of which I have treated, for the sake of simplicity), I shall, if he will confer with me through the address of my publisher, be only too pleased to correspond with him.

THE END.

www.ingramcontent.com/pod-product-compliance
Lightning Source LLC
Chambersburg PA
CBHW030756230426
43667CB00007B/991